AGATON SAX
AND THE
COLOSSUS OF RHODES

Also available in the Target series:

AGATON SAX AND THE DIAMOND THIEVES
AGATON SAX AND THE SCOTLAND YARD MYSTERY
AGATON SAX AND THE BANK ROBBERS
AGATON SAX AND THE CRIMINAL DOUBLES
AGATON SAX AND THE LONDON COMPUTER PLOT

in preparation:
AGATON SAX AND THE LEAGUE OF SILENT EXPLODERS

AGATON SAX AND THE COLOSSUS OF RHODES

NILS-OLOF FRANZÉN

Illustrated by Quentin Blake

TARGET

Target Books is a division of Universal-Tandem Publishing Co., Ltd., 14 Gloucester Road, London SW7 4RD

First published in Sweden by Stockholm. Alb. Bonniers Boktryckeri, 1966
and in Great Britain by André Deutsch, Ltd., 1972

First published in this edition by Universal-Tandem Publishing Co., Ltd., 1975

ISBN 0 426 10815 9

Printed in Great Britain by The Anchor Press Ltd., and bound by Wm Brendon & Son Ltd., both of Tiptree, Essex

Contents

I

Crime across the wires

The time has come to tell the full story of the awful crime that was committed, not so very long ago, right under Agaton Sax's nose—or, more precisely, ear.

The truth can no longer be hushed up. Reports have already appeared in certain leading newspapers in London and New York, but since they appear to be based on rumours, we have decided to tell the whole story right from its frightful beginning.

It was a beautiful May morning. At six thirty, Agaton Sax, editor-in-chief of Sweden's smallest (and best) newspaper, the *Bykoping Post*, entered the editorial office on the first floor of his house.

He expected the next few hours to be busy. He had several columns to write for his paper, and there would probably be the usual interruptions—news of a crime that called for his immediate attention, for example.

By seven he was writing an article insisting that something should be done about the disgraceful condition of the ancient bicycle stand outside the Public Library.

At seven thirty he phoned the Manager of the Local Dairy, asking him to explain, if he could, why their Chocolate Ice Cream was always so strongly flavoured with vanilla that it was almost impossible to eat, and to say what he proposed to do about it?

At seven forty-five, having got no satisfaction from the manager, he wrote sixty lines denouncing the practice of manufacturing uneatable ice-cream.

At eight he consulted his computer, Clever Dick, about the activities of an extremely dangerous gang.

At eight thirty he was able to despatch the following telegram to the Head of INTERPOL (International Police Force):

I HAVE SOLVED THE MYSTERY STOP ARREST ALL EXCEPT CHARLIE SQUEALER STOP HE HAS ALREADY BEEN ARRESTED IN MONTEVIDEO STOP AGATON SAX.

At eight forty-five he settled down to write another article for his paper, this time under the heading:

SOMETHING MUST BE DONE TO STOP THE INTOLERABLE RUSTLING OF TOFFEE PAPERS IN BYKOPING CINEMAS.

At nine-o-clock precisely a telephone call came through from Inspector Lispington of Scotland Yard.

Agaton Sax lifted the receiver.

'Yes?'

'Hullo!' said a voice in English. 'Is that you, Mr Sax?'

'Of course. Who else would I be?'

'Oh good! Splendid! This is Lispington speaking. Are you all right, Mr Sax?'

'Fine, thank you.'

'Just as I hoped! I am glad to hear you in such good spirits.'

'What about you, Mr Lispington?'

'I'm a little better now, thank you.'

'You haven't been ill, have you, Mr Lispington?'

'No, no, Mr Sax. Not ill, no no, not ill at all.'

'Your voice doesn't sound quite the same as usual,' said Agaton Sax, his round face suddenly assuming an expression of extreme watchfulness, as he pressed the receiver closer to his ear.

'Well, I am . . . a bit giddy,' said Lispington, and he did sound rather strange.

'Giddy?' exclaimed Agaton Sax. 'Have you . . . are you . . . ?'

'The dentist,' said Lispington.

'Have you pulled out a tooth?'

'Not me, no, but the dentist did. Well, as a matter of fact, he didn't *pull* it out, he sort of *sawed* it off, if you see what I mean, and then he put in another one.'

'Aaaahhh . . .' sighed Agaton Sax compassionately.

'That's exactly what I said—word for word.'

'Did you say he put in a new tooth?' Agaton Sax asked. He didn't feel as casual as he sounded.

'Yes. He said that I must try out the new tooth for about a week. After that, if it was comfortable, he would fit it permanently. What I have at the moment is a temporary fitting, he told me, just for the time being.'

'I see.'

Agaton Sax sat silent for a minute or two. His brain was working at high speed. At last he asked:

'Why?'

'Why?' repeated Lispington. 'Why what?'

'Why this temporary fitting, as he called it?'

'Because the tooth has to be tried out in my mouth for about a week. I must decide whether I like its shape, its taste, and so on. And then the permanent fitting will be done in Rhodes, of course.'

'In Rhodes, of course,' Agaton Sax echoed, as if he was not sure what Lispington had said.

'Yes, in Rhodes.'

'Rhodes. You mean the island in the Mediterranean?'

'Yes, of course,' Lispington answered casually.

'I see. You have to go all the way to Rhodes to have this tooth permanently fitted—is that it?'

'Yes, of course. Since there is a dentist there.'

'Why "of course"? Is this dentist in Rhodes the only dentist who can fit your tooth properly? Is that what you mean, Mr Lispington?'

'Of course not! There are hundreds of dentists who could do it, including the one who put this temporary one in yesterday.'

'I see,' said Agaton Sax, who was now beginning to understand. 'Then what is it you are trying to tell me, Mr Lispington?'

'Ah,' said Lispington, leaning back in his revolving chair, 'I bet you would like to know why I'm going to Rhodes?'

'But you just told me, didn't you?'

'Ha ha! Now listen carefully, Mr Sax, and I'll tell you the truth. If I have to go to the dentist in Rhodes next week, it's only because I shall be there anyway. And why shall I be in Rhodes next week? You have heard, of course, of the Colossus of Rhodes. *I am on his track!*'

This time it was Agaton Sax's turn to lean back in his chair, a satisfied smile on his round face.

'You are on his track?' he repeated, gently stroking his elegant moustache.

'Yes!' said Lispington triumphantly. You do *know* about the Colossus of Rhodes, don't you, Mr Sax?'

'Of course,' said the Swedish super-sleuth. 'Everyone knows that the Colossus of Rhodes was one of the Seven Wonders of the Ancient World—a huge bronze statue of the sun god Helios which stood astride the harbour of Rhodes. In 224 B.C. it was destroyed by an earthquake, and no trace of it has ever been found.'

'Quite right,' said Lispington. 'But there is more to it than that. Much more! Can you hear me clearly if I whisper?'

'Yes,' whispered Agaton Sax.

'Good. Someone might overhear us. Can you still hear me if I whisper like this?'

'Yes,' Agaton Sax whispered, even more softly.

'Hullo!' said Lispington alarmed. 'Are you there? I can't hear you! This is a rotten line! Are you there?'

'Yes!'

'Good. I think I'd better whisper in our secret code. Have you the cipher book with you, Mr Sax?'

'No, but I have it in my head. Go ahead.'

'Good,' answered Lispington. 'I'll use Code No. 54 C, backwards. You follow me?'

'I do.'

Lispington lowered his voice once more.

'Krefdevnioatar prodhughyridif ipreighueven gnash! Nor efghor klodustryb! Klyghu-cropping?'

'Klaroghilophrysine!' whispered Agaton Sax.

'Kliutryv eskthrados. You follow me? Hutjytredoss how!'

'How?'

'How? Asefrughestronoklefdot!'

'Asefrughestronokrevtod?'

'No, not Asefrughestronokrevtod, I said Asefrughestronoklefdot!' Lispington whispered with great emphasis.

'Oh, that's different,' answered Agaton Sax, leaning back and lighting a big cigar. 'You frightened me, Mr Lispington! Kilophrokodotus?'

They were now speaking so quietly that neither of them could hear properly what the other one was saying.

Suddenly the English operator broke in.

'Are you still speaking?' she asked.

'Krijufgh! Krijufgh what!' whispered Lispington in a scarcely audible voice.

'I'm sorry, sir? Did you say something? Are you still on the line?'

'Yes!' whispered Lispington angrily. 'Can't you hear we are? Krijufgh salamander!'

'Are you trying to be funny, sir?' said the operator, now even angrier than Lispington. She rang off abruptly.

'Dash it all!' whispered Lispington. 'She interrupted my chain of thought. Where was I?'

'You had just said that you said Asefrughestronoklefdot,' whispered Agaton Sax, puffing furiously at his third Monday cigar.

'That's it! Exactly! Jhegharaklefgahnas myvdes! Myvdes! Myvdesagha quick! Myvdesaghahjicla quicker!'

'Incredible!' said Agaton Sax. 'Absolutely fantastic!' Since it is strictly forbidden to reveal the codes used in conversation by Lispington and Agaton Sax, I have no authority to explain the complicated 'key' of this Code, No. 54 C, backwards. The best I can do is to translate it for you. This, then, is the gist of their conversation:

'Can you guess, Mr Sax, what I have discovered? There is a gang leader nicknamed the Colossus of Rhodes! I got wind of him all by myself. *You* have never heard of him, I'm sure!'

'Of course I have! As a matter of fact, I have been following his crimes with interest for more than a year.'

'Really? In that case, maybe we ought to co-operate? What about it? I am in top form!'

'In top form?'

'Yes! I'm going to strike at once!'

'Alone?'

'Well, yes, that was my intention. But you are welcome to join me, Mr Sax.'

'That's better. You almost frightened me, Mr Lispington. What's your plan?'

(Here followed the operator's distracting interruption.)

'I look forward to being decorated when I have caught the Colossus. I ought to be made a member of the Most Noble Order of Crime Busters. A magnificent order! Second class at least—perhaps even first class.'

You will have noticed that Lispington carefully avoided answering Agaton Sax's question as to *how* he intended to catch the Colossus.

'This case promises to be a very interesting one,' Agaton Sax whispered.

'I'm glad you think so.'

'But you must have a plan of action by now.'

'Ghokloptrectsuvets! Of course I have! Can you hear me, Mr Sax?'

'Yes.'

'Good. Listen carefully.'

Lispington lowered his voice. Agaton Sax did indeed listen carefully, very carefully. He was immensely curious to find out how much Lispington knew about the Colossus of Rhodes. Agaton Sax himself knew practically everything and had already made plans to take this remarkable criminal into custody some time in May.

'Can you hear me, Mr Sax? Good. Hjuludughaklackfodomis donkey . . . klyghsdha . . . No—now what's happening?'

'What is it?'

'Mofaghasdutryp huppla!' whispered Lispington. 'Someone is coming! Salamander!'

'Someone's coming? Salamander?'

'Yes.'

'Where?'

'Through the door. Ssshhh!'

'Who is it?'

'I don't know. Quiet! The door is opening slowly. What on earth? Hjkalughfhdrustrup? Katudruyfghephkan lost? Salamander!'

'I beg you, Mr Lispington, tell me what is happening!' urged Agaton Sax.

'Ssshhh! He can hear me!'

'You mustn't put up with this, Lispington! People can't just walk into your room.'

'What are you doing?' said Lispington in his usual voice.

'Me?' said Agaton Sax.

'No, I'm speaking to the man who has just come through my door. Salamander!'

'What's he doing?'

'I like your cheek, sir,' shouted Lispington, on the point of losing his temper.

'Be careful!' warned Agaton Sax. He could hardly bear the suspense.

'Can you believe it, he's locking the door on the inside!' said Lispington. 'You there—what do you think you're doing? Who are you, anyway? Salamander?'

'I'm from the cleaning company, sir.' A husky voice answered.

'Take care, Lispington!' said Agaton Sax. 'He isn't from the cleaning company. I can tell by his voice.'

'Don't try to fool me,' said Lispington angrily. 'No cleaning company would send anyone like you. Who are you?'

'Take it easy, sir. My company fixes locks as well as doing cleaning. My first job is to repair the lock on your door, and then I'll take down the curtains.'

'He is not a locksmith,' whispered Agaton Sax.

'You are not a locksmith,' repeated Lispington. Then he cupped his mouth and whispered to Agaton Sax: 'Kjyghetradghan dgfpemethinks? Now I understand! Ha ha ha! Salamander!'

'What do you understand?' moaned Agaton Sax. Lispington was at his most dangerous when he thought he understood something.

'Don't you see!' said Lispington with a laugh. 'It's a joke! It's rag day for the students here today. I had quite forgotten! This is just a student rag!'

'What makes you think that?' said Agaton Sax coldly.

'Ha! ha! ha!' Lispington chuckled softly. 'Because he's wearing a black mask.'

'A black mask?'

'Yes! I can see it quite clearly! Ha ha ha!'

'Very funny,' whispered Agaton Sax. '*Detryafgiskalon dgryas!* (This may be very dangerous—far more dangerous than you think!) Mr Lispington, can you hear me?'

'Of course!' said Lispington, gently circling in his revolving chair. 'I was a student myself, once. One year, just before the Christmas vacation, we dressed up as bean stalks! Can you imagine—bean stalks! Hyghtryfodsurts salamander!'

'For the last time, Mr Lispington, I warn you!' Agaton Sax was now on the verge of despair.

'Have no fear, Mr Sax!' Lispington answered cheerfully. But isn't it odd, how old some students are nowadays. Perhaps this chap is a lecturer who enjoys taking part in rag day stunts?' Pleased with this idea, Lispington turned to the stranger.

'Do sit down, won't you, and we'll have a chat about the good old days! Just let me finish this telephone call.'

The voice, no longer husky but peremptory and clear, answered with three well-known, ominous words:

'Stick 'em up!'

'Wait a minute, old chap,' Lispington called out. 'I can't hear you while I am on the phone.'

'Stick 'em up, I said!' repeated the voice.

'Now wait a minute, you should know better than to point a pistol at someone, even if it is unloaded. Put away that revolver.'

'I've had enough of this,' said the voice.

'If you don't put that weapon away immediately, I'll report you to your Principal,' said Lispington, no longer amused.

'And if *you* don't stop blabbing, you old nincompoop, I'll . . .'

Agaton Sax was at his wit's end. The situation was as bad as it could be.

'Haven't you got an alarm button under your desk?' he whispered urgently.

'Stop that!' said the voice. 'Hands on top of the desk.'

At that moment there was a knock on Inspector Lispington's door. It was only a feeble tap, but could it mean that relief was on the way? From the silence in the room Agaton Sax could tell that the intruder was listening intently. Lispington, taking advantage of the interruption, whispered into the phone: 'Fyghdestrihonslow kradusila?' (Can you warn my boss?)

'Shut up!' cried the voice.

There was another knock and the masked man put his ear to the door.

'Is that you?' he said. 'Good, I'll unlock the door. Come in as quickly as you can.'

To his dismay, Agaton Sax calculated that at least three more men were now in Lispington's office. The voice issued orders—one after another with bewildering speed.

'Lock the door! Pull the curtains! Give him a sleeping

pill! Shut him up in the vault! Search this office—go through it with a tooth comb!'

'Kadghufklomnos! Yup!' (Hurry up, please!) whispered Lispington to Agaton Sax. A second later the masked man snatched the receiver from his hand.

'Hullo!' said a voice that was obviously used to being obeyed.

'Hullo!' answered Agaton Sax, and his voice had even more authority.

For about seven seconds neither of them broke the silence. Then Agaton Sax continued. 'So it's you, Herr Gustaffson. I thought it was. I recognize your methods. And since I heard last week that you had just . . . left prison, I drew my own conclusions.'

The man in Lispington's office seemed to gasp for breath.

'Agaton Sax!' he whispered, and a terrible pallor spread over what could be seen of his face beneath the black mask. At the same time the other crooks either shook like leaves or froze into statues.

'In person,' said Agaton Sax with imperturbable calm. 'Listen to me, Herr Gustaffson! I know that in your own way, you are an artist in the world of crime. Nevertheless I wish to warn you: whatever else you may do—never harm Inspector Lispington!'

The silence which followed this solemn warning was broken by Lispington himself, who called out:

'Goghughysklasmun kjidefgas put! Salamander?'

Herr Gustaffson, cold, calculating, possessor of a masterly brain, who operated only at the highest levels of underworld activity, was almost paralysed when he realized that Agaton Sax had taken action to thwart his latest crime before he had even had time to commit it. How could this be possible? He, Herr Gustaffson, had planned everything down to the smallest detail. How could Agaton Sax possibly be aware of his most secret plans?

At this moment tension broke the nerve of one of the crooks. Unable to bear the strain any longer he rushed to the telephone, shouting into the receiver at the top of his voice: 'We're not afraid of you, you and your Agaton-dfhukladtrhs-asses and your Sax-ghus-silly-pigs! Your ghrush-silly-fatty-Sax talk doesn't frighten us! Ha! Ha! Ha!'

With that he hurled the telephone to the floor.

2

Telephones and red tape

Agaton Sax drew deeply on his cigar. His right ear still buzzed with the terrible invective levelled at him. He put the receiver carefully down on the desk beside the telephone so that the connection with Lispington's office in London should not be broken.

He was not afraid that his friend would come to any harm. Herr Gustaffson always avoided violence. But one thing was certain: within the next few minutes Lispington was going to be kidnapped.

Agaton Sax could see it all. Every detail of Gustaffson's plan fitted the theory he had worked out. The Colossus of Rhodes, Lispington's bad tooth, his journey to Rhodes, the dentist waiting for him on the island, Herr Gustaffson's daring stroke. Everything fitted in, everything was as clear as daylight to Agaton Sax—except for one or two minor points that need not bother him now. He knew exactly what to do. The only question was—would he have time to do it?

Fortunately, there were two telephones on his desk. He found both of them essential in his daily work, then even when he was speaking to someone on one phone, an urgent call could be put through on the other. While he was talking to the police in Paris, some appalling crime might be committed in London, New York, or Tokyo, or Bykoping, which would make it necessary for the police to consult him immediately.

He lifted the receiver of the second telephone, and asked Miss Olsen at the Bykoping Exchange to put through an emergency call—maximum priority—to Scotland Yard.

Miss Olsen knew what that meant. Barely one minute later, the London operator answered.

'Scotland Yard. Can I help you?'

'Listen carefully,' said Agaton Sax. 'This is Agaton Sax. Do you recognize my voice?'

'No, sir, I don't, I'm sorry.'

'Do you know who I am?'

'You just told me, didn't you?'

'Yes—but do you know *who* Agaton Sax is?'

'Don't be silly, sir!' said the girl, laughing. 'Of course I do. You are the man with the angry aunt.'

Agaton Sax sighed impatiently.

'Listen carefully,' he went on. 'You must get this right. It is extremely important. I have just had a call from Inspector Lispington. *He is in danger!* Get a General Alarm ordered throughout Scotland Yard!'

'A General Alarm, sir?'

'Yes! Don't you know how to do it?'

'Of course I do, sir. I just ring up the duty officer in the Alarms Section and . . . '

'No, no! The alarm button is right in front of you, on the wall above the switchboard.'

'I know, sir, but we are not allowed to touch that button. It's strictly forbidden. I must put you through to extension 1313.'

'No, don't, for Heaven's sake!' Agaton Sax protested.

But in vain. The girl had realized that delay would be dangerous, and had acted accordingly.

In the pause that followed Agaton Sax heard another voice—also a woman's.

'Agaton! Are you there?'

It was the wall of his office, or, to be more precise, it was the speaking tube that connected Agaton Sax's office with the kitchen.

'Yes,' he answered, through a cloud of cigar smoke.

'You are ten minutes late already, Agaton. If you don't come down, I'll have to come up to you.'

'No, wait.'

'But I've been waiting for ten minutes.'

'Who do you want to speak to?'

This time the voice came from Scotland Yard.

'I am Agaton Sax.'

'As if I didn't know!' shouted Aunt Matilda.

'Hullo!' said Agaton Sax, trying desperately to keep in touch with Scotland Yard.

'I can't hear you very well.'

'Then there must be something wrong with the wall again,' said Aunt Matilda angrily.

'What's going on?' said the voice from Scotland Yard.

'Agaton Sax here! Can you hear me now?'

'Of course I can hear you, Agaton! Why are you speaking English to me?'

'We must have a crossed line,' shouted the Scotland Yard voice. 'I can hear several voices. Who's there—how many are you? You'd better make up your mind who's going to do the talking, because I can't talk to half a dozen people at once. I can hear some foreigners talking, too, and some foreign language. What is going on? I don't like it at all!'

'Listen carefully,' begged Agaton Sax. 'Sound the General Alarm immediately. A gang of masked men has got into Inspector Lispington's office. He is in great danger! Do you hear me?'

'Sure I can hear you, whoever you may be. Do you think that people can ring up Scotland Yard when they feel like it and order a General Alarm as if they were ordering fish fingers and frozen spinach from the grocer's?'

'Don't you know who Agaton Sax is?'

'No, I don't! But I intend to find out who *you* are, take my word for it!'

'So you refuse to give the General Alarm?'

'Certainly, I wouldn't dream of doing any such thing.'

'Put me through to your boss. Now. At once!'

'So that's the game, is it? A really funny man, aren't you? It won't take five minutes to have this call traced and then we'll teach you to stop hard-working citizens from getting on with their jobs!'

Click! The line went dead.

'Aunt Matilda!' shouted Agaton Sax in his sergeant-major's voice. 'I don't want to be disturbed.'

He picked up the other phone, the one that was lying on his desk, still connected to Lispington's office.

'Hullo, is anyone there?' he asked.

Did he hear a whisper of sound, rather as if someone was

standing by the phone and holding his breath in an effort to hear without being heard?

'Hullo!' said Agaton Sax again. 'Is that you, Herr Gustaffson? If it is, listen to me, for this is your final warning, your last chance to reform, to become a useful member of society. Remember that you can never get the better of me. Think how I trapped you in Bykoping a couple of years ago, had you clinging precariously to the top of a fireman's ladder while I drove you to the police station. Think of the long lonely years in prison. Back out now, turn over a new leaf while there's still time.'

There was a hissing noise. Someone drawing breath through his teeth.

'Clumsy lout—silly old fatty Sax!'

Now this was definitely not Herr Gustaffson (who was always extremely polite) but one of his coarse, uncivilized henchmen.

Agaton Sax picked up the other phone. This time, one of Scotland Yard's golden voiced operators asked him politely, 'What can I do for you, sir?'

'I want the Superintendent, please. It's exremely urgent!'

'Just a minute.'

Another gentle voice came over the line.

'This is the Superintendent's secretary. I'm sorry, the Superintendent is in a meeting.'

'Interrupt the meeting! We've only seconds left. Inspector Lispington is in danger!'

'I'm sorry, but the Superintendent's not in the building. His meeting is in the city.'

'Then let me speak to his deputy, please,' said Agaton Sax, showing admirable patience.

'Just a minute, sir.'

Not just one minute. Several minutes.

'Hullo. Deputy Superintendent's office here.'

'Can I speak to the Deputy Superintendent at once, please. It's a matter of life and death!'

'I'm sorry, he's in a meeting with Chief Inspector Briggs.'

'Then give me Chief Inspector Briggs, please!'

Agaton Sax sounded so determined he was almost hypnotic. Anyone would have felt compelled to put him through to anyone he wanted.

'Chief Inspector Brigg's office,' answered a pleasant female voice.

'Can I speak to him, please?'

'I'm sorry, he's in a meeting with the Deputy Superintendent.'

'I know, but this is extremely important!'

'I'm so sorry, but they're not here. The meeting is in Chief Inspector Brown's office. I'll have you transferred.'

Agaton Sax lit his fourth cigar.

'Chief Inspector Brown's office.'

'I know that he's in a meeting, but please let me have a word with him.'

'I'm so sorry, sir, the meeting was cancelled half an hour ago. Can I put you through to any other meeting?'

'I want Chief Inspector Brown, not a meeting!'

'I see, well unfortunately he is in another meeting—with the Superintendent. I'll put you through.'

'But the Superintendent's meeting is in the city.'

'If you think I can put you straight through from this office to another number in the city, sir, you are absolutely wrong. I'll have you transferred to the Superintendent's office.'

Half a minute later Agaton Sax was answered by a man, a man who was panting a little, as if he had been running.

'So sorry, sir, but I had to answer another phone first. I'm afraid they've put you through to the wrong department, sir. This is Lost Property, and we only concern ourselves with things, objects, as it were, and never with people. You know what I mean, things you lose in trains, buses, taxis, aeroplanes, helicopters and so on. So if this Mr Carmichael—that's the name of the missing person you are enquiring after, isn't it?—well, if he has really disappeared—and you never really know, you know, with people who other people think have disappeared. In my position you've got to be extremely careful when you receive a report saying that someone has disappeared, because, well, you know how it is, some people just want to lie low for a while, they haven't really *disappeared* at all. If you want to report the disappearance of this Mr Carmichael, you must do it properly and fill in a form first. If you want to know how to get through to the Forms Department, ask for Section B. No, sir, no trouble at all. What's that you say, sir? He hasn't disappeared? Then why the . . . Are you trying to be funny, sir? Are you denying that you rang me up to report the disappearance of a Mr Carmichael? And now you are trying to tell me his name is Lispington. No, sir . . . Oh no, not me, sir . . . You're going to talk to the Forms Department whether you like it or not, I know your sort, a troublemaker, that's what you are . . .'

A few seconds later, another voice answered: 'Forms Department here, Section B. You want to speak to the Superintendent? What makes you think he is here?'

'I know he isn't there, but somebody put me through to you before I could stop them,' said Agaton Sax, by now so furious that he pitched his newly lit cigar out of the window.

As he did so he had a sudden brilliant idea, one of those flashes of inspiration without which even the cleverest detective is lost.

'This is a warning,' he said. 'The Forms Department is

threatened by four masked men who are at this moment planning to steal five thousand copies of Form CA 754.'

'What did you say?' the voice betrayed the fear felt by its owner. 'Did you say CA 764?'

'No, CA 754.'

'Good Lord! Our best form, and brand new, we haven't had a chance to issue one yet. Of all the confounded cheek, this is . . . '

'What are you going to do about it?' asked Agaton Sax cunningly.

'I'll give the General Alarm immediately, of course!' said the man, spitting with rage.

'Good man! I knew I could trust you.'

'You bet you can!'

But, unfortunately, this official, courageous enough to act on impulse, had not reckoned with the cautious attention to regulations shown by other departments. It soon became clear that no one had any intention of letting him give the alarm until he had gained the necessary permission from someone in authority.

At last Agaton Sax said, 'Don't worry, I'll see what I can do. Just get me put through to the switchboard again.'

'Very good, sir. Good luck to you—I'll do anything in my power to protect my forms.'

Once more Agaton Sax heard the operator's voice.

'Switchboard. Who do you want to speak to?'

'A senior official. I don't mind who.'

'Do you want to report a crime, sir?'

'I certainly do.'

'What sort of crime, sir?'

'Kidnapping!'

'Good gracious! Where, what district?'

'Scotland Yard.'

'Yes, sir, this is Scotland Yard—but *where* did this kidnapping take place, sir?'

'In your building—in Scotland Yard! Hurry up, please, there's no time to lose.'

There was silence for a moment. Then the operator spoke.

'So it's you again!' (She was very angry now.) 'I thought I recognized your nasty voice! You're the hoaxer who rings up every Monday reporting all sorts of impossible crimes. Last Monday, you tried to tell me that you had painted the statue of Eros yellow, the Monday before that you said you had stolen the Crown Jewels, and hidden them in some old ketchup bottles in Greek Street. Now you've got some far-fetched story about people being kidnapped in Scotland Yard! You ought to be ashamed of yourself, a grown-up man and all. I'll report you to the police!'

She was so angry that her voice broke and she couldn't go on. Agaton Sax lit another cigar. It gave him another bright idea. This time he couldn't fail, thanks to his extraordinary skill as an impersonator.

When the next operator answered, he said cheerfully:

'Good morning! This is Inspector Lispington—I'm sure you recognize my voice?'

'Of course! Good morning, Mr Lispington.'

'I just wondered, as I'm calling from home, and you would expect me to be at Scotland Yard by now. I must speak to someone in the Conference Room on the fourth floor.'

'Certainly, Mr Lispington, just a minute, please.'

At last!

'Conference Room. Inspector Smith speaking.'

'Listen, Inspector Smith, this is Agaton Sax. Do you recognize my voice?' (Agaton Sax was now speaking normally.)

'I'm sorry, I don't. But if you can tell me how many finger prints we had in our Finger Print File on the first of January, 1972, I'll know you are Agaton Sax.'

What an intelligent man, thought Agaton Sax. Aloud, he said: 'You had 20,365 on the first of January, 1972. By last week, you had added a further 1,567, of which 949 were British.'

'Correct in every detail,' said Inspector Smith. 'You must be Agaton Sax.'

'Your conclusion is quite correct, and does credit both to your intelligence and your good judgement,' said Agaton Sax pompously. 'Now listen carefully to what I have to say. Give the General Alarm immediately! Inspector Lispington is in danger. Herr Gustaffson and three of his gang are in his office preparing to kidnap him.'

'Herr Gustaffson? Good Lord! Hold on, please, I'll be back in a second.'

Agaton Sax glanced at his shot-proof wrist watch. Almost eleven minutes had passed since he first tried to get the alarm raised. Would this clever Inspector Smith be in time?

At last he heard the Conference Room door open, and

quick steps crossing the floor. Then an excited voice almost shouted into the receiver: 'Too late, Mr Sax! Lispington's room was empty. All the drawers have been searched, the safe had been forced open and all the papers in it removed or torn to pieces. Lispington himself is nowhere to be found. We are checking all the exits and we've sent out a General Alarm call to every police station in Europe. What a dreadful business. How did you get involved, Mr Sax?'

'I had a call from Lispington,' said Agaton Sax and gave the Inspector a brief account of the events which you have just followed in detail.

Inspector Smith drew in his breath.

'This is the worst thing that's happened since Lispington was appointed an Inspector,' he murmured to himself.

'Don't worry,' said Agaton Sax. 'You'll have him back within a week.'

3

Clever Dick in danger

What a failure!

Agaton Sax paced up and down the room, brooding on the blow which Herr Gustaffson (born Chihuahua, Mexico, probably on 3rd May, 1930) had just dealt him, and, of course, Scotland Yard.

Only the reappearance of the Colossus of Rhodes could be more dangerous than this, Herr Gustaffson's latest coup.

The Colossus of Rhodes—not the bronze statue of the ancients, but the modern gang leader of the same name—had so far successfully baffled all the police chiefs of Europe (and their secret agents). Everyone knew his real name was not Colossus. But what was it? Who was he? Where was he? That was easy, in Rhodes. But how did they know he was in Rhodes? The answer was, they didn't know, they only guessed. What made them decide on Rhodes? Because four of the richest millionaires in the world had recently been robbed of approximately 9 per cent of their fortunes when, carelessly enough, they had sailed into the harbour at Rhodes in their luxury cruisers. Priceless necklaces, gold evening slippers, snuff-boxes, and platinum ash-trays had disappeared from safes and wardrobes. Each time the hapless owner had discovered his loss, he had found a tiny scrap of paper on the floor, and with the aid of a magnifying glass, had been able to read the following message: THE COLOSSUS WAS HERE.

To quote just one example of his ruthless behaviour. One of the richest men to be found in Southern Europe, Alcibiades Croesus, sailed into Rhodes one day in his yacht, *Crock of Gold*, and dropped anchor. At 8.30 in the morning, Alcibiades Croesus, dressed for breakfast, was sitting in his cabin, waiting for his manservant to enter with the tray. As usual when he was on holiday, he was looking forward to counting up his cash. He produced his wallet. Knowing that he had spent seven shillings the day before, he calculated that he ought to have £972,999·65 left. Imagine his disappointment when he found his wallet empty except for a scrap of yellow paper with the mysterious words quoted above written on it: THE COLOSSUS WAS HERE. No, just a minute, there was more writing: P.T.O. With trembling hand Alcibiades Croesus turned the paper, and through his diamond-studded magnifying glass, read the following words: SEE YOU AGAIN SOON.

It's not hard to guess what happened next. Mr Croesus inspected his safe. It was empty. How much money had there been in the safe? Mr Croesus himself was quite certain it was £10,780,000, but his chief cashier swore there had been only £10,775,000.

For the past year, Agaton Sax had been following the activities of this remarkable crook with great interest. As long ago as 1st April he had said to himself: This has got to stop. Something must be done, and *I*, Agaton Sax, will do it. That is why he had been so alarmed to hear that Lispington intended to do something about it. Now, everything had changed. He had three important tasks to tackle: to save Lispington, to sieze the Colossus, and to catch Herr Gustaffson, who had been at large for about two weeks, that is, about a fortnight too long.

With a bound, Agaton Sax leapt from his chair and went over to the curtain which hung in front of the wardrobe door. Pulling it aside, he pressed a small button marked COME, and stood for 4·5 seconds, silently waiting for his computer, Clever Dick, to reach its operational position in the wardrobe from the coal-hole where it remained safely hidden when not in use.

Clever Dick was indeed a masterpiece of technology, his own brain child, and capable of making calculations beyond even his powers—a feat to which Agaton Sax gave his ungrudging admiration. Moreover, the incomparable Clever Dick could answer questions, give advice, and issue instructions in any situation, no matter how dangerous or complicated it might be. For this reason it was essential that the computer could accompany Agaton Sax on all his travels, so he had built it in two parts, each easily portable and weighing only fifty pounds.

Agaton Sax tore his gaze away from his beloved Clever Dick and with Aunt Matilda's sewing machine oil lubricated all the most important parts of the complicated machinery.

Then he went to work. It is well known that a computer must be 'fed' with facts so that it can function. Once you have given it the information to work on, it will give you the right answers.

Agaton Sax now 'fed' Clever Dick with everything he knew about Herr Gustaffson. He did this by pressing several yellow, red, and green buttons, and by pulling a number of handles and levers. Then he tapped out the following question on the computer's typewriter :

'What will Herr Gustaffson do, now that he knows that I, Clever Dick, am on his track?'

Clever Dick went to work with speed and determination. Within seconds he had solved several thousand complicated intellectual problems and made a long series of calculations.

After only half a minute, a green light flickered on the instrument panel and a type-written paper emerged through a slot in the computer's panel.

Eagerly, Agaton Sax grabbed it and read the following:

AWFULLY CRITICAL SITUATION. HERR GUSTAFFSON A CRIMINAL GENIUS. A MOST DANGEROUS MAN. WARNING.

That was all right so far as it went, but it was not enough. Agaton Sax stroked his moustache thoughtfully, then fed the computer a few more facts. Clever Dick answered immediately:

99 PER CENT PROBABILITY HERR GUSTAFFSON TRY DESTROY ME, CLEVER DICK. HERR GUSTAFFSON MASTER OF SILENT METHODS. MUST BE STOPPED. WARNING.

This was serious. Agaton Sax looked at his watch. If the computer was right in saying that Herr Gustaffson would try to destroy it—then it was reasonable to assume he would act on the spot. He must be ready tonight to fool an attack by Herr Gustaffson himself or some of his assistants.

Silent methods, Clever Dick had said. What did he mean by that and what silent methods could Herr Gustaffson be contemplating to silence Clever Dick?

He fed the computer still more questions. Clever Dick's answer was a list of seventeen different methods which Herr Gustaffson might use. Agaton Sax read it slowly, then listed them in order of probability. Then he asked Clever Dick to do exactly the same thing, and smiled with pleasure when the answer showed that Clever Dick's order of probability coincided exactly with his own. You could really trust this computer, its judgement never erred.

He leapt to his feet with a sudden burst of energy. In just ten minutes he had collected together a hundred or so mechanical and electrical gadgets and packed them in a big suitcase. With surprising agility for one so portly he slid down the fire escape—choosing this exit rather than the stairs and the door, in order to avoid Aunt Matilda's eagle eye—and started work in the garden, or rather among the trees in the garden. His preparations took him about half an hour.

He was now as hungry as a hunter, and headed for the kitchen. It was empty, Aunt Matilda having disappeared. He heard her footsteps above, for she had at last succeeded in getting into Agaton's office, making furious assaults with her duster upon the desk, the book-shelves, and the piles of paper stacked all over the room.

Agaton fetched a couple of eggs from the larder, and made himself a nice little omelette.

Just as he was about to swallow the first mouthful, he heard Aunt Matilda's voice from the office. He switched on the speaking tube and listened attentively to her words, which pierced the air like arrows.

'Agaton! Are you there?'

'Yes, Aunt!'

'Something horrible is happening. Can you hear me?'

Agaton Sax stood up, throwing his napkin on the table.

'What is it, Aunt?'

He was deathly pale.

'Agaton—the confuser—Clever Nick, he . . . he . . . he has started talking!'

'What on earth do you mean, Aunt?'

'I mean what I say. He has started to talk—or to think aloud. This is going too far, Agaton! I won't stand any more of it.'

'But it's impossible, Aunt. Clever Dick can't talk, neither can he think aloud.'

'Oh, can't he? Well I've just told you he can. Listen Agaton! Listen to him, talking and talking, just like one of those politicians in Parliament who don't know when to stop.'

Agaton Sax pressed the speaking tube to his ear and listened intently. With a sudden thrill of fear he realized that his Aunt was right. There was a voice in his editorial office—a deep, authoritative voice speaking passionately, as if in anger.

'What can be happening?' he murmured, almost staggering. Then, shouting into the tube 'I'm coming,' he dashed through the door and up the stairs in three huge leaps.

He wrenched open the door of his office. There stood Aunt Matilda in the middle of the room, stiff and straight, pointing her duster in solemn accusation at Clever Dick, whose green eye glittered in the open door of the wardrobe.

'Hear for yourself, Agaton! Listen to him carrying on!'

He listened, and what he heard froze his blood, for Clever Dick was making a solemn declaration.

'This is intolerable! I can't put up with this sort of humiliation any longer. First he asks a lot of silly questions, and when I answer them to the best of my ability, he doesn't take a blind bit of notice of what I have said. The whole situation is impossible! He's completely incompetent! He knows nothing, he understands nothing, and yet he struts about like a peacock! I shall take the matter up at the May meeting of the Street Planning Committee, and then if nothing is done I'll lodge a formal complaint with the chairman of the Town Council, and demand that the whole matter be referred to the Drafting Committee.'

'Now, Agaton, you can hear for yourself what a nincompoop you've got in your wardrobe,' said Aunt Matilda angrily. 'Is it likely that Clever Nick, or whatever you call him, is going to attend a meeting of the Street Planning Committee? I never heard such nonsense—what does he know about street planning? What a mess you have made of things this time! How do you think the Town Council would feel if a machine came marching into their offices, shouting about the chairman of the Town Council and laying down the law about a lot of other things he doesn't understand.'

Agaton Sax listened patiently until his Aunt had finished. He was quite calm again.

'Aunt,' he said, 'don't upset yourself, nothing is wrong. But I must remind you that I have warned you many times, never touch any of the buttons in this room. Not one of them.'

'I haven't touched any buttons.'

'You have—this one.' And Agaton Sax pointed to a pale green button on the wall, near the wardrobe door. 'You must have flicked it with your duster.'

'Quiet, Agaton! He's starting again. Now he's got two voices. Listen!'

It was true, Clever Dick did seem to have a second voice, which remarked: 'But you'll have to prepare a thorough financial report first. Figures, you know, always impress the committee. They will want a complete breakdown on costs.'

'But everybody knows what costs are involved.' Clever Dick's first voice answered sharply.

'Come over here, Aunt, and I'll show you,' said Agaton Sax, taking Aunt Matilda by the arm.

From the window, he pointed to the pavement which ran beside the garden of the Bykoping Post Office.

'Look,' he said.

Aunt Matilda saw two men deeply engaged in conversation.

'What about them?' she asked.

'Don't you recognize them? It's Berg and Andersson. It's *their* voices you can hear, not Clever Dick's,' said Agaton, pressing the button on the wall.

The voices ceased. Aunt Matilda lowered her duster and turned a suspicious eye on her nephew.

'Then how do you explain that Berg and Andersson are speaking with Clever Dick's voice?' she said, irritably.

'They are *not* speaking with Clever Dick's voice,' Agaton Sax explained. 'Clever Dick hasn't got a voice. They have nothing to do with him. Listen and I'll explain everything. Clever Dick is in danger. This very night a gang of masked men will try to destroy him. That's the reason why I mounted microphones in the trees. Everything the crooks say as they come through the garden will be heard by me in this room. Now, you inadvertently switched on the loud-speaker in here and that's why we heard what Berg and Andersson were saying on the pavement. Now I have switched it off. It's not very nice to eavesdrop on other people's conversations—unless they happen to be crooks,' he added under his breath.

'If Clever Dick is in danger, why don't we take him up to the attic, where they wouldn't notice him becaust it's full of old junk and rubbish, as you well know, Agaton. There's that old motor-cycle of yours which would *not* run on water, as you thought it would, or that wretched vacuum-cleaner you designed, which worked the wrong way whenever it felt like it and sprayed dust all over the room instead of sucking it up as any self-respecting vacuum-cleaner would.'

At the memory of this awful incident, Aunt Matilda shook the duster so violently that Agaton was forced to stop her with a peremptory wave of his right hand.

At the same time, the gleam of an idea came into his eyes. His Aunt's words about the vacuum-cleaner had given him one of those brainwaves which had made him so successful in the fight against crime.

'I've got it,' he shouted. 'Thank you, Aunt! Now I know how to save Clever Dick!'

This conversation was followed by several hours of intense preparation, including making mathematical calculations, installing technical equipment and putting through telephone calls and telex messages. First of all, he rang the Electricity Board and had a long conversation with the manager. Then he phoned Scotland Yard, and after that contacted the airport authorities in Stockholm, the capital of Sweden, about a British monoplane which he expected to arrive in Bykoping that same evening.

The man at the airport dealt with Agaton Sax's request as if it were just a matter of routine. 'Your instructions will be carried out in full, Mr Sax,' he said. 'We are always happy to be at your service, as you know. Thank you, sir.'

In dangerous situations, in fact most of the time, Agaton Sax's appetite always improved. Aunt Matilda had to prepare four ham sandwiches, six cheese sandwiches, several boiled eggs, coffee, and meringues. At sixteen thirty he got into his sports car, and drove to Johansson's meadow. A fifty foot high outlook tower had been erected in a wood beside the airstrip. It was the property of the Ministry of Works, the Treasury, the Forestry Department, and the Bykoping branch of the committee for the Preservation of Aesthetic Values. Agaton Sax had a permit to use the tower whenever he wanted, issued jointly by all the above bodies. From it he had an excellent view of Bykoping and its environs, particularly because a powerful telescope was mounted on the observation platform.

At twenty thirty-five his long vigil was rewarded when he spotted a small monoplane which circled the suburbs of Bykoping for a few minutes, then made a pinpoint landing on Agaton Sax's private runway. Two men leapt from the aircraft.

'French Jules and Hopeless O'Donovan,' said Agaton Sax to himself. 'Exactly as I thought. They have been specially trained for this kind of secret mission.'

The two crooks worked fast. Agaton Sax watched them closely, for it was vital that he should know for certain what equipment they had brought. Just what he'd expected. They unloaded two bicycles and a machine which looked like a collapsible fire-tender designed for easy reassembly. Then they went back into the plane.

'They won't attack until after midnight, probably about one o'clock,' Agaton Sax thought to himself.

He stayed in the tower until twenty-three thirty, using the telescope to watch the two men moving about in the plane. Then he climbed swiftly down, went to his car and took his own bicycle from the boot. He had the same reason for bringing his bicycle as French Jules and Hopeless O'Donovan had for bringing theirs—the need for moving fast and silently.

He rode swiftly through Bykoping's silent streets, noticing that even the windows of the post office were dark. He propped his bicycle carefully against the kerb, and crept into the garden to check that everything he had prepared earlier was still working.

Everything was in order. He tiptoed up the stairs to the editorial office.

The moon had passed behind a cloud and the room was pitch dark. He stood at the window behind the curtain watching the garden. What a fatal night this could be. Everything depended on his ability to guess the full extent of Herr Gustaffson's dark plan, this stage of which he had entrusted to French Jules and Hopeless O'Donovan, and which they were about to carry out in the still of the Bykoping night.

At one o'clock he heard footsteps. The crooks had left their bicycles by the gate, and Agaton Sax could make out that they were each carrying half of the machine which resembled a small fire-tender.

The footsteps ceased. The microphones which Agaton Sax had rigged among the trees were so sensitive that he could hear every whisper from the garden.

'Have you got the plan of the house and garden?' French Jules whispered to Hopeless O'Donovan.

'Yes, here it is.' Hopeless O'Donovan produced a large paper.

'Where's old Fatty's room?' asked French Jules.

'It's the one marked nine,' said Hopeless O'Donovan.

'You're quite sure? Which way do we go, then?'

'To the right.'

'Right! Keep your eyes open, we're walking a tightrope, you know.'

They approached the house cautiously. Agaton Sax was on tenterhooks, for he couldn't understand why they had turned right.

'Is this the door,' whispered French Jules.

'Yes.'

'But it's open!'

'Well?'

'Don't you find that rather odd? I smell a rat.'

'A rat? Here?' Hopeless O'Donovan said nervously.

They crept into the house, and their voices died away, but only for a few seconds. Agaton Sax had installed mini-microphones throughout the house, so that he could hear every footstep they took and every word they whispered.

A vague feeling of unease stole over him. Had he, after all, made a mistake in anticipating the details of their plans?

'There's something fishy about this,' muttered French Jules.

'Why?'

'Why? Don't ask me. Think! Do you really suppose that old Fatty lives in his own wine-cellar?'

'Ought he to live in someone else's wine-cellar?' asked Hopeless O'Donovan hopelessly. 'Can you see the computer anywhere? Switch on the torch, will you!'

There was a moment's silence, while French Jules played the torch over the cold, damp walls of the cellar.

'I tell you this is a trap!' he whispered suddenly. 'Let me see that map.'

Hopeless O'Donovan handed him the map, which he studied impatiently. Then he groaned:

'You thick-head. You read the map upside-down. The wine-cellar is six, not nine. What do you think Herr Gustaffson would have said if we'd gone back and told him we'd wrecked a couple of dozen bottles of Burgundy instead of Clever Dick? We want the real room nine, which is upstairs. Come on!'

They were in the garden again. Agaton Sax had carefully locked the door leading to the ground floor. In a few seconds, French Jules, an expert in the art of paying uninvited visits to the rich, had picked the lock and opened the door. They felt their way up the stairs to the editorial office.

Agaton Sax heard them coming, and darted into the room across the landing, locking the door after him.

Through the keyhole he saw them steal into the editorial office, lighting their way with a torch.

'There!' whispered French Jules. 'There it is, in that doorway. Clever Dick, your hour has come! Wait a minute,' he warned his companion, who was eager to get started, 'we'd better make sure it's safe. Fatty is as cunning as a fox.'

French Jules searched every corner of the room before he set to work.

'O.K.,' he said at last. 'You see that power point in the wall over there? Two hundred and twenty volt alternating current—right? We'll rig the machine and plug it in.'

Hopeless O'Donovan obeyed. He was efficient, and a fast worker. Agaton Sax could see the machine clearly now. It had a big hose with a broad mouth-piece.

'O.K.,' said French Jules once more. 'We'll put it here. That's it! Steady now! Are you ready?'

'Yes.'

But just as French Jules went to switch on, a terrifying voice broke the silence:

'BEWARE! I AM CLEVER DICK! I AM DEADLY DANGEROUS! BEWARE!'

The two crooks shrank back, pale as two ghosts. Hopeless O'Donovan clutched the handle of the machine with shaking hands, while French Jules, the tougher of the two, bit his lip.

'Get going!' he muttered threateningly.

But now the horrifying voice was heard again :

'BEWARE! BEWARE! YOU HOLDING THE MACHINE ARE HOPELESS O'DONOVAN AND YOU STANDING BESIDE IT ARE FRENCH JULES. I KNOW YOU. YOU WERE SENT HERE BY HERR GUSTAFFSON. BEWARE! BEWARE! ANYONE WHO TRIES TO WRECK ME, CLEVER DICK, IS NOT AS CLEVER AS HE THINKS. HE'LL BE CAUGHT AND JAILED.'

Hopeless O'Donovan was now trembling so violently that he let go the handle of the machine. French Jules, a ruthless and reckless criminal, snatched the hose from Hopeless O'Donovan's hand, hissing contemptuously :

'Coward!'

'YOU'LL BE CAUGHT!' Clever Dick's voice had a sinister, metallic ring.

'But you'll be caught first!' shouted French Jules, defiantly switching on the fire-tender and aiming the mouthpiece straight at Clever Dick.

Now, at last, the hateful computer would be destroyed! The fire-tender was filled with a liquid called tricloretylenfenolftalinhydroacetondilutine (with a dash of petroanalysisdissolutionhydrocine). This mixture—*Herr Gustaffson's Special*—has never been equalled when it comes to destroying delicate machinery, TV sets, air-craft engines, computers, and so on. The machine itself was practically noiseless, but nevertheless the power of the jet was so great that the liquid could force its way into the very heart of the most elaborate machine and destroy it so completely that it was impossible to say, after the operation, what it had originally been designed for.

A diabolical smile lit French Jules' face as he felt a slight trembling in the handle and knew that the engine was working.

But a cruel disappointment awaited him. No jet of liquid

came from the mouthpiece. He shook the hose. The engine was working, there was no doubt about that, then why was nothing happening?

'Caramba!' he exclaimed in Spanish, picking up the hose in order to examine it.

There was a cry of despair. The mouthpiece had got caught in his jacket. He tore wildly at it to free it, but in vain. What a disaster if the liquid should squirt out on to his new jacket.

And yet—what a minor disaster that would have been compared to what was really happening! How could French Jules know that the engine was working in reverse! In other words, it was not spurting out liquid, it was sucking in air like a vacuum-cleaner.

'Caramba! Caramba! Hopeless O'Donovan! Come here and help me get rid of this cursed mouth-piece. For Heaven's sake, do something!'

As if Hopeless O'Donovan wasn't doing something! His teeth were busy chattering with fright all the time.

'I *knew* there were ghosts!' he murmured feebly, trembling like a leaf. 'I knew it even when I was a child, though my mother used to laugh at me! I wish she was here now to see for herself!' Hopeless O'Donovan had no intention of helping French Jules, as quick as a flash he slipped out of the door, tumbled down the stairs, and flung open the back-door.

But he forgot to reckon with Aunt Matilda and the Bykoping Police Force, represented by Sergeant Antonsson. They were waiting on the other side of the door. Aunt Matilda had prepared a yellow plastic pail filled with cold porridge, and with a steady and experienced hand she poured the porridge over Hopeless O'Donovan's unsuspecting head. After this he was even more useless as an accomplice of Herr Gustaffson's than he had been before. It only remained for Sergeant Antonsson to handcuff him.

Meanwhile, French Jules was dancing about all over the floor, desperately trying to free himself from the ruthless mouthpiece of his own wonderful machine. Suddenly he heard Clever Dick's voice again:

'YOU BRAINLESS IDIOT! TAKE OFF YOUR JACKET, AND YOU'LL BE A FREE MAN!'

French Jules' hair stood on end when he heard intelligent advice coming from a mere machine. However, he pulled himself together, tore off his jacket and flung it on the floor together with the hose and mouthpiece.

But it was too late! With a shudder of dismay, he saw the door open.

'Bad luck, French Jules,' Agaton Sax said. 'This is journey's end for you.'

And the look he gave French Jules was more terrifying than any gun.

4

Ups and downs

When French Jules and Hopeless O'Donovan had been securely locked up, Agaton Sax explained to Aunt Matilda and Sergeant Antonsson what had really happened.

'I asked the Electricity Board if they would be kind enough to switch the current in Bykoping into reverse for a couple of hours. You probably had no idea that this could be done, but it can. Anything worked by electricity can be reversed. You can make a petrol pump suck up the petrol from a tank instead of filling it, or films in the cinema and on television run backwards—this can be extremely annoying, particularly in the case of detective stories; vacuum-cleaners can be made to spray out the dust they took in yesterday instead of sucking up today's. It was Aunt Matilda who gave me the idea. Of course, the Electricity Board didn't exactly jump at the suggestion that they should reverse the current, because it was almost bound to cause breakdowns here and there, but since I only wanted it done for an hour or two in the middle of the night, they finally gave in.'

'You are going to cost the tax-payer a lot of money,' Aunt Matilda remarked sternly.

'About £1,000, I imagine,' said Agaton Sax, 'but Scotland Yard will pay. It was an absolutely vital part of my overall plan, because I knew those two would be armed with some deadly gadget that would do its work silently and efficiently. I did manage to soften them up though, before delivering the knock-out blow. I made them believe that Clever Dick could talk. This was another idea I got from you, Aunt Matilda. I installed a microphone in the room next to my office, and put a loud-speaker inside Clever Dick. Then all I had to do was distort my voice so that it sounded metallic—just as Clever Dick might sound.'

'Are you trying to tell me that he really can speak?' asked Antonsson, terrified at the prospect.

'Oh no. I mean, I tried to sound exactly as Clever Dick would sound if he could speak. The rest, you know.'

Agaton Sax then went to bed and slept soundly for seven hours. He awoke refreshed and set about preparing Clever Dick for a long journey. He dismantled him, and carried the two halves to his new plane, *Hermes 2*. Then he went to the bank and drew out several hundred thousand Greek Drachmas. Next he looked in at the newsagent, where he chose three guide books on Rhodes. Finally he phoned Scotland Yard and asked for news of Lispington—but there was none.

Aunt Matilda made him enough sandwiches to keep him going for twenty-four hours, and his preparations were complete. Before setting out he sent the following telegram:

TO SUPERINTENDENT SMITH SCOTLAND YARD STOP LISPINGTON WILL BE BACK SHORTLY STOP DON'T SEARCH FOR HIM IN LONDON STOP THE COLOSSUS OF RHODES AND HERR GUSTAFFSON WILL BE SENT TO YOU UNDER ARREST WITHIN A WEEK STOP PLEASE INFORM THE *WORLD BANK* AND THE *INTERNATIONAL ASSOCIATION FOR THE MUTUAL SUPPORT AND ASSISTANCE OF MILLIONAIRES (IAMSAM)* THAT THEY NEED HAVE NO FURTHER FEARS STOP AGATON SAX.

Having said good-bye to Aunt Matilda, he drove his sports cars to his private runway on Johansson's meadow and checked all the instruments in *Hermes 2*. As he took off it was exactly 8.50.

An hour later, he was in radio contact with ground control in Copenhagen.

'Are you Mr Sax from Bykoping? Over.'

'Yes. Over.'

'Destination Rhodes? Over.'

'That's right. Over.'

'We have an important message for you. Over.'

'From whom? Over.'

'From a lady. Over.'

'Her name? Over.'

'She refused to tell us. She said you would understand. Over.'

'I do. Over.'

'Will you take the message? Over.'

'Yes, I'm listening. Over.'

'It wasn't exactly a message. She just said you would understand. Over.'

'That's right. I do. Over.'

'You do understand? Over.'

'Yes. Over.'

'Very well—that was all. Thank you. Over.'

'Thank you. Over and out.'

With a little sigh, Agaton put his hand into his pocket. Just as he thought! There was a small plastic tube containing twenty preponhinyldiatosinperkaminalstreptomangalhydrophicine pills, he had to remember to take one after each meal. Aunt Matilda had put the pills there.

The distance between Bykoping and Rhodes is so great that it is impossible for a small plane to do the journey without re-fuelling at least once. Agaton Sax intended to make a brief landing at Budapest in Hungary. But something happened that upset all his plans.

Over the little town of Barth in Northern Germany he suddenly felt so hungry that he decided to switch on the auto-pilot (which navigated the aircraft by itself) and make his way to the baggage compartment at the back of the plane, where both Clever Dick and Aunt Matilda's hamper were stowed away. Rubbing his hands together in anticipation of the meal he was about to enjoy, he took out the hamper, lifted its lid (inscribed with the words TO AGATON SAX, A GIFT FROM THE SWISS POLICE) and removed the cloth, under which he expected to find two veal cutlets, four sandwiches (one each of ham, cheese, *pâté de foie gras*, and salami), a peach and a small bag of meringues.

He looked into the basket, and his eyes narrowed. Only a few small traces of the sumptuous meal that Aunt Matilda had prepared for him remained: two cutlet bones, well picked, some sticky brown pulp, all that was left of the beautiful peach, and a few grains of meringue.

In spite of the doleful sight which confronted him, Agaton

beamed with delight and his eyes shone with pleasure, for his dachshund, Tickie, was crouched in a corner of the hamper. Tickie, who must have secretly followed his master into the car, crept into the plane, and finally wormed his way into the hamper, to be rewarded by the discovery and consumption of its extremely interesting contents.

Tickie was well fed and happy. To show her gratitude she wagged her tail gently and lifted up her head. Agaton Sax bent down and, scratching her behind the right ear, murmured to himself, 'Good girl . . .'

But the sight of the basket and the thought of what it had contained, made him even more hungry. He glanced at his watch. He would put down in Hamburg for an hour or two and get a bite to eat.

He went slowly back to the cockpit. As he sat down, he spotted a small white dot silhouetted against the blue sky a few miles behind him. It was another plane, following the course he was flying on. Nothing could be more natural, but Agaton Sax was always on the alert, even when he was in the air. He observed the other plane closely through his telescope, and noticed that it was exactly the same model as *Hermes 2*, kept the same altitude and the same speed.

He banked sharply to the right, climbing about two hundred yards. A few seconds later the other plane made exactly the same manœuvre. Only one explanation was possible: he was being followed. He made up his mind at once what course of action he would take. Fifteen minutes later, he touched down at Hamburg. Having passed through all the necessary controls, he ran across the central hall to a window from which he could see the runway where he had landed a few minutes earlier. He was just in time to see the other aircraft land, and through his pocket telescope he spotted a man hurrying from the plane. Who was he? Herr Gustaffson—naturally.

Agaton Sax had already decided on his plan of action. He walked briskly up to the information desk, where passengers can send or receive messages. He handed the girl behind the counter two small pieces of paper, and asked her to read the messages on them over the loudspeaker system, so that they would be heard in every lounge and waiting-room. Then he went to a call box, from which he could see anyone enter or leave the central hall.

Two minutes later, Herr Gustaffson came into the hall. He held a handkerchief up to his nose in an attempt to hide his face, and he looked round very cautiously. At that moment, the girl on the information desk read out the following message:

'Attention, please! Will Mr Agaton Sax of Bykoping in Sweden please come to the information desk to receive an important message. Mr Agaton Sax from Bykoping in Sweden. Thank you.'

She repeated the message twice. Herr Gustaffson had just sat down on a sofa. He was hiding his face behind one of his specially designed newspapers, which looked quite ordinary, but were actually equipped with almost invisible slits through which the reader could observe all that was going on around him. Agaton Sax could imagine him listening attentively to the message, and at the same time darting watchful glances here and there through the slits in the newspaper.

Agaton Sax walked out of the call box, making sure that Herr Gustaffson saw him. He went up to the information desk.

'I am Mr Sax,' he said. 'You have a message for me?'

'Yes, sir. It's from Scotland Yard.'

He took the message, which was, of course, the one he had given her a few minutes ago, and made a great show of reading it carefully, stroking his moustache, nodding as if well satisfied with its contents, and finally tearing the message to pieces. He dropped the fragments carelessly into a big ash-tray on the counter, lifted his hat politely to the information girl, and walked slowly away in the direction of the restaurant.

Herr Gustaffson immediately lit a cigarette, took a few quick puffs and strolled over to the ash-tray to stub out his cigarette—or rather, to pretend to do so. His real purpose was, of course, to pick up the scraps of paper left there by Agaton Sax. Having done so, he retired to a telephone box, put the pieces together, and read the following message:

FROM SUPERINTENDENT SMITH SCOTLAND YARD STOP TO AGATON SAX STOP YOU WERE QUITE RIGHT STOP HERR GUSTAFFSON IS ON HIS WAY TO ZAGREB STOP I'M COMING STOP SEE YOU AT THE GRAND HOTEL IN ZAGREB AT 21.00 HOURS STOP WITH MY WARMEST WISHES SMITH.

Herr Gustaffson rubbed his hands with delight.

Agaton Sax rubbed his hands, too. By means of one false message read over the loud-speakers, and an equally false telegram apparently sent by Superintendent Smith to Agaton Sax he had made Herr Gustaffson believe that he, Agaton Sax, was on the wrong track; that he was on his way to Zagreb, not to Rhodes. In other words, he had succeeded in lulling Herr Gustaffson into a dangerously false feeling of security. Herr Gustaffson himself was doubtless on his way to Rhodes, where Mr Lispington had already been taken by his accomplices. Herr Gustaffson was confident that he had nothing more to fear from Agaton Sax, who was safely out of the way on a false trail to Jugoslavia.

Agaton Sax had a quick meal.

This was a fatal mistake—the second mistake, in fact, that he had made in ten years: he let Herr Gustaffson out of his sight for about fifteen minutes. Such negligence cannot be excused.

When he got to the runway, ready to resume his flight to Rhodes, *Hermes 2* was gone, vanished into thin air. Herr Gustaffson had taken the wrong plane, that is to say, he had taken Agaton Sax's aircraft instead of his own.

What a knock-out blow! His first thought was to alert every airport in Western Europe, but on second thoughts he decided he could not possibly do anything so foolish. Why should he tell the airport authorities and police forces of Europe that he, Agaton Sax, had been outwitted so easily? Impossible! He chose the best alternative: he ran over to Herr Gustaffson's aircraft, checked the instruments, and within minutes had taken off in pursuit of his enemy.

The loss of *Hermes 2* was a trifle compared to the loss of its precious contents; Tickie and Clever Dick. He clenched his teeth and pulled the throttle full out as soon as he had left Hamburg behind him. Unfortunately, Herr Gustaffson's plane was slower than *Hermes 2*, which gave Herr Gustaffson a start of approximately an hour and a half over his pursuer.

By 21.35 he was approaching Rhodes. The sun had set, and he saw with a thrill the fairytale glitter of the lights of the town, and of the airport a few miles beyond.

He put the nose of the plane down in an elegant right turn, and managed a perfect landing, in spite of the fact that Herr Gustaffson's plane hardly came up to the standard of performance he expected. Just as the wheels touched the ground, he spotted *Hermes 2* on an adjacent runway. He permitted himself a quiet smile of satisfaction, because this was just what he had expected.

As he switched off the engine he looked up and saw ten police officers in smart uniforms standing on the runway some twenty yards ahead of him. He frowned, jumped out of the plane and hurried up to them. How awful if the Rhodes police had been quick enough to arrest Herr Gustaffson. That would be a severe blow to his grand plan to arrest Herr Gustaffson and the Colossus at the same moment.

'You haven't arrested Herr Gustaffson, I hope?' he asked in fluent modern Greek.

The officer in charge saluted him with solemn courtesy, and said, 'You are under arrest, sir.'

Agaton Sax stared at him. Then he saw the funny side and said with a smile, 'That's all right. I can take a joke.'

'I never joke when on duty, sir.'

'I'm in a hurry,' said Agaton Sax impatiently. 'Will you please tell me whether you have arrested Herr Gustaffson or not?'

'I just told you that *you* are the one who has been arrested, sir!'

'But I am Agaton Sax!'

'Kindly spare me your ill-timed jests,' said the officer sternly. 'Come with me, please.'

'I warn you!' said Agaton Sax menacingly.

'And I warn you, *Herr Gustaffson*!' the police lieutenant retaliated, nodding to his men, who immediately surrounded Agaton Sax.

'Agaton Sax arrived here an hour and a half ago,' he added coldly. 'He was in good order, and so were his passport and all his other papers. His aircraft was in good order too. You can see it over there.'

'That aircraft is mine,' said Agaton Sax. 'Herr Gustaffson stole it from me in Hamburg, and all the papers he showed you were forged—as forged as his passport. Here is *my* passport.' A sudden thought struck him. 'By the way—how do you know the plane I was flying belongs to Herr Gustaffson?'

'Scotland Yard sent us a telegram containing a detailed description of Herr Gustaffson's plane. Since you were flying the plane, you must be Herr Gustaffson.'

'Listen,' said Agaton Sax. ' I really am in a great hurry. Have you ever heard of the Colossus, sir?'

'Yes,' said the officer, and added triumphantly, 'I have reason to believe that you are he, sir! You may be using an honest Swedish name, Herr Gustaffson, but you haven't fooled us. We've caught you at last, and almost in the act! You'd better come with me to the station.'

Agaton Sax summed up his chances. If he accompanied the police to the station, it would probably take him at least ten hours to convince the conscientious lieutenant that he was really Agaton Sax. It took him just five seconds to make a decision. The stakes were high, but the game was worth it.

'Listen, sir,' he said amiably. 'I only want to save all of us from disaster, and you in particular from making the humiliating mistake of arresting and imprisoning Agaton Sax—a nightmare for any ambitious police officer jealous of his reputation. I want to make a bargain with you. If I can convince you that I am Agaton Sax, I promise never to tell anyone about the mistake you have made. You, in return, must promise never to tell anyone that Herr Gustaffson managed to steal my plane. In other words, if what has happened here today should ever leak out it will be equally embarrassing for both of us.'

'And how can you prove that you are Agaton Sax?'

'Easily. You have just told me that *Hermes 2* belongs to Agaton Sax. If I can show you something inside the plane that only Agaton Sax would know about, will you believe me?'

'O.K.,' said the officer and walked, with his men, over to *Hermes 2*.

Agaton Sax's plan was simple.

'May I begin?' he asked, opening the door. Then he whistled, and called, 'Tickie! Tickie!'

In a moment, Tickie was in his arms, happily licking his carefully trimmed moustache. The police officer and his ten constables saluted them solemnly.

'Rare dog, rare master, as we say in modern Greek,' the officer said. 'You are undoubtedly the owner of the dog. Consequently, you must be Agaton Sax and cannot be detained any longer. The secret we share will always be a secret kept by us both.'

'Thank you,' said Agaton Sax warmly. 'And now for Clever Dick.'

Saying this he dived into the plane, and found the two parts of his computer untouched, which didn't surprise him in the least. Herr Gustaffson had been sure that French Jules and Hopeless O'Donovan had destroyed Clever Dick —consequently he had never thought of looking to see what might be hidden under the big green tarpaulin at the back of the plane.

The same three difficult tasks still lay ahead of him: to find and rescue Inspector Lispington, to identify and sieze the Colossus, and, last but not least, to arrest Herr Gustaffson and his gang.

5

Underground reunion

The first thing you must do when you arrive in Rhodes on the sort of mission that Agaton Sax had undertaken is to disguisc yourself. There are quite a few possibilities to choose from, but it's a good rule to make yourself as different as possible from your usual self. If you are tall, then you try to make yourself appear as small as you can, if you have a moustache, you shave it off, if you have a green moustache, you dye it blue, and so on. Agaton Sax increased his height considerably using a device which he had designed and made himself, and which he called *The Agaton Sax Shoe Raiser*. He then put on the most appropriate false beard to be found in his collection, and dressed up in Tyrolean costume, the final touch being a green hat with a red feather. He was staying at the Grand Hotel, where (having first obtained permission from the Rhodes police) he registered himself as Herr Strauss from Vienna.

He took his strongest shot-proof torch and set off for the centre of the town, accompanied by Tickie. The streets were full of tourists, and nobody seemed to take any notice of the somewhat exotically dressed stranger. He strolled along looking as calm and relaxed as any ordinary sightseer. But his calm was only on the surface, inside he was on fire with excitement, because he knew that within a matter of hours he would confront his enemies, and that a decisive battle would be fought.

After a while he reached the Old Town, in which stands the famous Palace of the Grand Master—one of the most massive castles in the world. It has a deep, broad moat and high walls with gigantic towers. He approached one of the entrances to the castle, but seeing a sentry watching the gate, he retreated, and turned into a narrow lane. On his left he saw a dilapidated house.

Suddenly Tickie pulled at her lead, sniffing eagerly at something on the ground.

She has scented a rat, he thought.

Tickie pulled harder on her lead, and Agaton Sax let her have her head. She dragged him into a small yard, in which there were several large piles of stone and mortar.

'It can't be a rat,' he thought, 'because if it were, Tickie would growl.'

At the far end of the yard, there was a stone wall with a large, dark hole in it. Moonlight penetrating the foliage of two acacia-trees lit up the wall and the hole, and Agaton Sax realized suddenly that he was in fact facing the castle wall. Through this hole, it would almost certainly be possible to gain entrance to the castle itself.

Tickie was obviously most anxious to explore the unfamiliar ground inside the hole. She gave Agaton Sax one of those looks which meant that she wanted to tell him something, then pulled urgently on her lead again.

Agaton Sax understood that his intelligent little dog had picked up an interesting scent. They made their way into what proved to be a very dark passage, about three yards across and two and a half yards high. It sloped slightly downwards.

This must be an underground passage leading to the moat, he thought, as he played his torch on the rough stones.

Suddenly Tickie stopped, pricking up her ears and growling. 'Sshh!' whispered Agaton Sax. 'We must keep absolutely quiet.'

Tickie understood. They moved cautiously forward. He switched off the torch, and they groped their way in complete darkness, Tickie's right side rubbing against Agaton Sax's left leg.

The silence was broken by a faint banging that seemed to come from somewhere beyond them in the darkness—or perhaps from the street above their heads? Tam-ta-ra-ram-ta-ram-tam-ram . . . An almost inaudible, regular knocking, like a drum, or someone wielding a pickaxe, or perhaps the rhythmic throbbing of a machine left for somc obscure reason abandoned in the darkness.

Several theories flashed through his mind—but none seemed to offer a reasonable explanation of the strange noise. This was certainly one of the darkest mysteries he had come up against. In his long struggle against crime he had found it absolutely necessary to learn pretty well everything about all kinds of noises, and he had collected, recorded, and carefully indexed 11,078 noises in all. He had divided them into several main categories: human noises, animal noises, machine noises, sounds made by earth, fire, water, and so on. His collection contained every conceivable kind of noise, large and small: vintage cars of various ages, tropical butterflies, washing machines and washing-up machines, school children (infant, junior and senior school), printing presses for evening and morning papers, knitting needles, running water at different temperatures, board of directors' meetings, post office queues, counterfeit money presses, rusty hinges on doors in London and other cities, gum-chewing, crowd reaction to scoring in cup matches (goals and penalty goals) to mention just a few.

But this was a sound he had never heard before, nor

recorded. It seemed to be a strange mixture of human and animal noises. But could that be possible? Could it be a robot that had lost its way in this underground passage beneath the castle of Rhodes? A robot that had suffered some kind of a mental breakdown and was now tramping the darkness, vainly trying to escape?

Agaton Sax felt something like a shiver run down his spine. With the utmost caution he groped his way along the wall, attempting to distinguish something in the enveloping dark. There! Suddenly he saw a feeble light—a pale, green eye staring at him.

He advanced another ten steps along the passage. A shape was outlined—it seemed to be connected with the green eye, but it was half hidden, for at this point the passage curved slightly.

He stopped abruptly, silencing Tickie by putting his hand across her mouth.

It was not a robot, nor a ghost. It was a man. He had wedged a torch in to a crevice in the wall, which threw a dim light over the man and the mysterious green eye.

The man had not seen Agaton Sax, who hesitated a moment while he made up his mind what to do next. The noise was now much more distinct. It came from something which looked rather like an ordinary box, except for the green eye, which still glowed palely in the darkness.

The man was making strange gestures with his right arm—every now and again he stretched out his hand as if to touch the box and whenever he did this, the noise increased in volume.

Still unnoticed by the man, Agaton Sax moved closer.

The man was dressed in Turkish national costume and had a square-cut, black beard.

Agaton Sax gripped his torch, and assessed his next move.

If he . . . ? No, he must wait one more minute. He must be absolutely sure before striking.

The man lifted his hand again and Agaton Sax was now close enough to see him open a small door in the front of the box, put his hand in, withdraw it, and finally close the door again.

There didn't seem to be any explanation for this strange behaviour. Agaton Sax did not usually find it hard to under-

stand things that were incomprehensible to others. But this time he was baffled. On the other hand, he was sure he knew the answer to the most important question of all.

Confidently, he switched on his torch and directed the beam directly into the man's eyes. The man staggered, took a step backwards and pressed himself against the rough wall of the tunnel. At the same time, his right hand flickered to his pocket as if to pull out a revolver.

'Stop!' Agaton Sax commanded, in a voice that is recognized and feared throughout the underworld.

The man staggered again.

'Who are you?' he cried hoarsely.

'Who are *you*?' retorted Agaton Sax.

'I asked you first!' said the man, who had overcome his first terror and was now showing signs of recovery.

'But I have tracked you down,' said Agaton Sax.

'Oh you have, have you? Then I warn you . . . !'

'Don't bother, my friend. You are powerless,' said Agaton Sax, enjoying his superiority.

'Not as powerless as you think!' the man answered. 'To begin with, you don't know the power of this device.'

Agaton Sax turned his torch and let the beam play on the strange box.

'The sooner you explain to me what you are doing here, and what is the purpose of the strange box-like equipment you are hiding, the sooner we can talk things over in an atmosphere of mutual confidence,' said Agaton Sax.

'There is no law against being in an underground passage with a piece of equipment, you know,' rejoined the man, now angry enough to be rude. 'I forbid you to disturb me in my important work!'

'And what kind of work is that, if I may ask?'

'Mind your own business! It's my work not yours!' shouted the man, even more angrily.

'Very well, answer this question,' said Agaton Sax haughtily.

'I don't have to answer any questions!'

'Don't you? I think you'll change your mind when you hear this one, sir. *Where is Inspector Lispington?*'

The man reeled and seemed to gasp for breath, his mouth twitched nervously so that his beard shook.

'How should I know?' he said at last, attempting to bluff it out.

At that moment a very strange thing happened. The greenish eye slowly went out, and another eye, a red one, glimmered in the darkness. The throbbing stopped. In the ensuing silence the man asked quietly:

'Why do you want Inspector Lispington?'

'Because I am determined to find him.'

'Why?'

'Because I am Agaton Sax!'

The man reeled again.

'Can you prove it?' he asked hoarsely.

'Look.'

And Agaton Sax tore off his false beard.

'Agaton Sax!' cried the man. 'You *are* Agaton Sax!'

'And you, sir, are Inspector Lispington,' replied Agaton Sax.

6

Micro-photography

'My dear friend!' the two men exclaimed simultaneously, after which Tickie gave vent to her joy by jumping up into Lispington's arms, and licking his face so vigorously that the glue fixing his beard in place dissolved and it fell off.

'This really is a happy surprise,' said Agaton Sax. 'I thought it would take me at least twenty-four hours to find you. It was Tickie who put me on the right track. She got the scent of your footsteps, knowing you, presumably, from your visits to Bykoping.'

'Good dog, very good dog indeed,' said Lispington, fastening his false beard back on to his chin again. 'As you know, I am very fond of animals. 'I'm deeply moved.'

'You must tell me all that has happened!' said Agaton Sax. 'How did you get to Rhodes, how did you manage to escape, and where is Herr Gustaffson? There are hundreds of questions I want to ask you.'

'I will explain everything, just as it happened,' replied Lispington with supreme composure. 'Shall we sit down? There are two big cannon balls here, relics of the sixteenth century. Please be seated, my dear friend!'

They sat down, and Lispington carefully placed one leg over the other, while Agaton Sax directed his attention to the mysterious box whose red eye still shed a feeble light upon the rough wall.

'I know that you are well acquainted with Herr Gustaffson,' said Lispington, 'an appalling rogue, and yet, in his own strange way, a gentleman of sorts. After my telephone connection with you had been broken, he made me swallow a very bitter pill, the name of which he didn't mention.

Then he bowed to me and said: ' "I apologize, Mr Lispington, for this intrusion, but I happen to know that you know a lot about the Colossus of Rhodes. I've got to find out what you know, and I've also got to take you abroad for a while. Will you be so good as to conceal yourself in your vault while I search your office?"

'One minute later, the pill had its effect on me,' Lispington went on. 'When I woke up again, I found myself in the smallest room I have ever seen. I wasn't tied up, but locked up so thoroughly that although I tried I soon realized escape was impossible. How long I was there, I don't know—perhaps five hours.'

'And then?'

'Then something most unexpected happened,' said Lispington. 'I really don't know how to explain it.'

'Tell me.'

'Well, I sat down on the bed, feeling sure that there must be some way of escaping from a locked room that no one had ever thought of. Suddenly I heard footsteps outside the door, and leapt to my feet. I heard an angry female voice shouting something in a strange language I couldn't understand at all—perhaps modern Greek or some other Adriatic language. Then suddenly she began to speak English.

' "Is there someone there?" she cried.

'Yes!

' "Where?"

'Here!

' "What are you doing in there?" she asked angrily.

'I don't know,' I replied truthfully.

' "Why don't you come out, then, you clot!" she replied in a very insolent tone of voice.

'Because I can't! They've locked the door! And I'm no more a clot than you are, madam!

'She rattled the door-handle, tampered with the lock and, a minute or two later, opened the door.

'There stood an elderly lady with a broom in her right hand. She stared at me, and I stared back at her. She said: "How do you expect me to do the room if you lock yourself in?"

'I didn't expect you to do the room! Where am I?

' "If you don't know where you are, sir, then you ought to be ashamed of yourself," she said in the same insolent voice. "The best thing you can do is to go home."

'How can I go home when I don't know where I am? I shouted. Now I was really angry.

' "You can go wherever you like as far as I'm concerned," she said, "so long as you hop it quick!" She really was very vulgar. Just imagine, Mr Sax! "hop it quick!" I flew into such a rage that that's just what I did, without even stopping to say good-bye or thank her for opening the door. I emerged into a narrow lane. The sun was overhead, and it was very hot. After I had walked through the streets for a while, it began to dawn on me that I was in Rhodes. I took a room at a hotel, and then went out to buy some Turkish clothes. All this happened only a few hours ago.'

'And you have seen no sign of Herr Gustaffson?'

'No.'

Agaton Sax had risen from his cannon ball and was racing backwards and forwards across the narrow passage in some agitation.

'And the cleaner?' he asked. 'Where did she go?'

'She went into the next room, I think, where she no doubt gave them a good scolding, too.'

'I see,' said Agaton Sax thoughtfully. 'Well, we've obviously no time to lose. But tell me one thing before we go, Lispington—what is this box thing for? And why have you . . . in short, Lispington—what *are* you doing here?'

'I'm testing this equipment,' said Lispington, pointing proudly to his red-eyed monster.

'But why here—why in this underground passage?'

'Because I was afraid to test it in my hotel room, in case someone came in.'

'I see, and this—er—apparatus, what's it for?'

'It's a P.C.M.'

'A P.C.M.?'

'Yes, of course! You don't mean to say, Mr Sax, that you can manage without a P.C.M.?'

'Of course I can,' said Agaton Sax with a rather superior smile. 'Is it a secret machine?'

'Oh no, it's not secret. I bought it in Rhodes today.'

'And what . . . what does P.C.M. stand for?'

'Paper Chewing Machine, of course!' exclaimed Lispington, surprised at his colleague's ignorance.

'But why? What do you want it for?' said Agaton Sax, irritated by the fact that Lispington had found a machine he couldn't identify.

'To destroy secret papers,' went on Lispington. 'If you burn secret papers, skilled criminal chemists can reassemble the ashes and read what was printed or written on them. But this machine chews all kinds of paper into a thick porridge that no chemist in the world, however skilled a criminal he may be, can read. Can you read porridge, Mr Sax?'

'And the two eyes?' asked Agaton Sax, ignoring the question.

'Elementary, my dear Mr Sax! When the green lamp is on, it means that the machine is hungry and wants more paper to chew. But as soon as it is full, that is to say when it has room for no more paper, the green light goes out, and the red one comes on.'

'I see.'

'There is another model, called the P.C.M.B. When it is full, it emits a discreet but quite audible belch. That's the model I prefer, but the Chief Cashier at Scotland Yard refused point blank to let me have it. It was too expensive, he said. Can you imagine, Mr Sax! The P.C.M.B. costs only seventy-five pence more than the ordinary P.C.M. I sent a telegram from here to the Chief Cashier, asking for permission to buy the P.C.M.B., and he replied with a cable saying: "PLEASE EXPLAIN WHY YOU WANT THE P.C.M.B. WHEN THE P.C.M. IS FIFTEEN SHILLINGS CHEAPER?" Now my first telegram cost £1. His answer cost 90p. I sent a further telegram explaining my views—that was £1·50. He replied with yet another telegram, insisting that for financial reasons I must buy the cheaper model. This telegram cost £1·20. So we exchanged telegrams costing £4·60, all to save 75p. The man is impossible!'

'No doubt,' said Agaton Sax. 'But we must get on now. Let's go to your hotel. I have some very important information for you.'

The two sleuths hurried out of the passage and, stopping only to allow Lispington to buy a bag of dog-biscuits for Tickie, made their way to his hotel. Agaton Sax told his colleague all about his adventures, and Lispington listened attentively, frowning with concentration.

'And now, Lispington,' said Agaton Sax as he finished his story, 'you must tell me about your tooth?'

'My tooth? Oh—my tooth! Well, it aches a bit.'

'Can you take it out?'

'Take it out?'

'Yes, if I remember rightly, you said it was only a temporary fitting and was to be replaced by a dentist here in Rhodes.'

'Oh yes, that's right,' said Lispington. 'I'd forgotten all about it. I'll go and see the dentist first thing in the morning.'

'Just a minute,' warned Agaton Sax. 'I'll have to have a look at the tooth first.'

'What?'

'I must have the tooth, please! I want to examine it closely.'

Lispington nodded in agreement and tried to pull it out. It was more difficult than he had imagined.

'A very well done job, I must say,' he muttered, trying once more.

'A pair of tweezers, perhaps,' offered Agaton Sax helpfully.

'Tweezers? I beg you, Mr Sax, to have some consideration for my feelings.'

'I'm sorry, Lispington, but this is extremely important.'

Lispington rang the bell and asked for a pair of tweezers to be brought to his room. A few minutes later he managed to pull out the tooth. He gave it to Agaton Sax, who took a beautifully designed pocket-microscope from his jacket and examined the tooth minutely.

'Just as I thought!' he exclaimed triumphantly.

'Are you a dentist as well as everything else?' Lispington asked tartly.

'No, but I know what teeth can be used for. As early as 1940, the well-known Swedish criminologist, Bo Willners, pointed out some of the uses to which criminals can put their teeth—or other people's teeth.'

'Criminals? Criminals in my mouth? What on earth are you talking about?'

'Just that. Mr Willners established that things can be smuggled in teeth or in fillings.'

He took a fine pointed instrument from one of his inside pockets, put a magnifying-glass to his right eye, and started to work on the tooth.

'Behold!' he said triumphantly. 'The Colossus!'

'The Colossus? In my tooth?'

Agaton Sax did not reply. Instead, he carefully pulled from the tooth an object which was so small that you could barely see it with the naked eye. Then he rummaged in his suitcase, and produced a developing and enlarging kit. He dashed into the bathroom, turned off the light, worked feverishly for a few minutes, and emerged holding in his hand a photograph the size of an ordinary playing card.

'There!' he said proudly. 'This is an enlargement of the micro-photograph that was hidden in your tooth. The dentist you visited in London put the photo in the tooth, and told you to make an appointment with a particular dentist here in Rhodes. *Both dentists are employed by the Colossus of Rhodes!*'

'How disgraceful!' Lispington exclaimed indignantly. 'Give me back my tooth.'

'In a minute. First we must study this enlargement carefully. You see what it is?'

'A map.'

'Exactly. A map of the underground passages where we met only an hour ago.'

He put the photograph on the table.

'Here, in the top right-hand corner you can see a big X. That's the spot where I believe the Colossus will be found.'

'The Colossus? The gang leader?'

'No, not the gang leader, the real Colossus, the gigantic bronze statue which was one of the Seven Wonders of the World and which vanished in an earthquake in 224 B.C.'

'That means it's been lost for some 2,196 years!' exclaimed Lispington. 'Do you mean to say that we have now found it in my mouth?'

'No. But the map is a micro-photo of an old drawing made in the sixteenth century and now in the possession of the British Museum. For centuries no one had given it a thought; then one day, quite recently, the Colossus got wind of it and began to think. He ordered his London agent —your dentist—to ask the British Museum to photograph the old map. As soon as your dentist received the photo, he reduced it and printed it on micro-film. It was this that he tucked into your tooth.'

'But why in a tooth? And why on earth in my tooth?'

'Simply because he knew that you were going to Rhodes.

He knew that you had been ordered by the police commissioner at Scotland Yard to go to Rhodes in pursuit of the Colossus. By using the two dentists in London and Rhodes, both his accomplices, he could get a copy of the map quickly and cheaply.'

'So the Colossus thinks he can find this famous old statue?'

'Yes. But that's only part of his plan.'

'I don't understand!' said Lispington angrily. He hated being out of his depth.

'Then tell me, Lispington, why did you go to this particular dentist and not to one of the other 10,500 or so dentists in practice in London?'

Lispington considered this question for a few moments.

'I remember!' he exclaimed. 'I got an advertisement through the post a few days ago, announcing that this dentist had set up in practice near Scotland Yard. *Attention!* it said—*Special Offer! For one week starting Monday, all Scotland Yard Inspectors will be given dental treatment at half price.* That's why I went to him. I seized the opportunity, and I saved twenty pounds.'

'Excellent.'

'I'm still not quite clear, Mr Sax. This Herr Gustaffson, is he a dentist, too?'

'No.'

'Then why did he kidnap me?'

'Very simple,' said Agaton Sax, dismissing the problem with a wave of his hand. 'Herr Gustaffson is the mortal enemy of the Colossus of Rhodes. Herr Gustaffson knows that the Colossus would like nothing better than to hand him and his gang over to the police. He found out that your cheap dentist was one of the Colossus's men. He shadowed you, and soon discovered that you were being sent to Rhodes in pursuit of the Colossus. At this point he made his first mistake. He decided that you and your dentist were working together and that the dentist had given you some incriminating evidence against him, Herr Gustaffson. That's why he took you prisoner and searched your office. But he was not familiar with Mr Willners' researches into the use of teeth as a means of smuggling, so he never dreamt that it would be possible for a micro-film of a map to be carried from London to Rhodes in one of your teeth.'

'Damn!' said Lispington. 'Double-damn!'

'Don't worry!' said Agaton Sax. 'Everything is under control now.'

'But why did Herr Gustaffson bring me to Rhodes?' asked Lispington, his curiosity still not quite satisfied.

'Because he needs *you* to arrest the Colossus and his gang. You see, Herr Gustaffson's plan is to track down the Colossus and help himself to the millions of pounds that he's stolen. Then he intends to tell you secretly where you can find the Colossus. You will then arrest the Colossus and, hey presto! Herr Gustaffson will vanish with the stolen millions. He's a clever one, he is.'

'And the Colossus? The statue, I mean.'

'I haven't finished yet,' continued Agaton Sax. 'With the aid of the map from your tooth the Colossus is sure he can find the Colossus. He has in fact suggested to Herr Gustaffson that their two gangs should join forces, dig up the statue, and share the profit they would get from selling it. But the Colossus, of course, is not above a bit of double-crossing either. He fully intends to denounce Herr Gustaffson, and have you arrest and jail both him and his gang.'

'What a fantastic story! This is double-dealing unprecedented in the history of crime!' exclaimed Lispington excitedly.

'Double double-dealing, you might say. Two gangs fighting each other and both pretending to co-operate while they are busy cheating each other. Both using you to put the other under lock and key, and both ready to make off with the money. But neither the Colossus nor Herr Gustaffson reckoned with me, Agaton Sax! How stupid they are!'

Lispington paced the room in a state of great agitation, violently puffing at his cigar. Suddenly he stopped, and thrusting his cigar in Agaton Sax's face, said, 'I haven't told you everything, Mr Sax!'

'Haven't you?' said Agaton Sax uneasily. 'You haven't taken any steps, I hope?'

'I have indeed. You'll be informed in due course.'

'Thank you, that will be splendid. But now we must get to work on the map.'

'The map?'

'Yes, you must not forget to go to the dentist with the map.'

'Are you going to let him have the map?' asked Lispington, shocked.

'He'll get *a* map,' said Agaton Sax. 'A different map, not this one. We'll draw a new map, a forgery, then we'll reduce it, and insert it into your tooth. Do you see what I'm driving at?'

'Of course!'

Agaton Sax set to work at once. He had an extraordinary talent for drawing maps, and for all kinds of photography; developing, printing, reducing, enlarging, masking and so on. In a very short time he had produced a brand new map, as small as the genuine one, placed it where it belonged, and given the tooth back to Lispington.

'Take this tooth to the dentist in the morning and tell him that it has fallen out and you want it replaced. But go carefully! You never know with dentists!'

Lispington nodded consent. As he popped the tooth into the right-hand inside pocket of his jacket, he felt something in one of his other pockets—a tiny object—no larger than an ordinary toffee—but extremely important.

'Do you know what this is?' he asked, with a rather pleased little smile.

'No!'

'It's a magnetic tape!' he announced triumphantly. 'I have made a priceless recording.'

'Excellent!'

'We'll listen to it tomorrow morning,' Lispington said mysteriously.

7

A greedy pelican and a strange language

On the following morning, Inspector Lispington went to the dentist. He had the dentist's address in his head, and the tooth in his pocket.

An elderly nurse opened the door.

'I want to see Dr Xambis,' said Lispington.

She gave him a searching look.

'Your name, please?'

'Inspector Lispington. I have a message from William S. Brown, my dentist in London. He recommends my teeth—or rather one of my teeth—to the attention of Dr Xambis.'

'I see. Please come in and sit down in the waiting-room. Dr Xambis will see you in a few minutes.'

She disappeared. A rasping noise could be heard coming from the dentist's surgery. Lispington turned white. Was Dr Xambis attacking a block of concrete with his drills and chisels? What was the meaning of those horrible hammer-strokes. What caused the frightful jarring that he could hear all the time? Whose were those muffled voices?

About half an hour later the nurse opened the door again.

'Will you come this way, sir,' she said in a voice which tried to sound friendly.

Dr Xambis was standing by the dentist's chair. He was a tall, muscular man, probably as tall and strong as any dentist to be found in Europe. Nothing could be seen of his face, for it was hidden behind a white mask.

'Please place yourself in the chair, Inspector Lispington,' he said in broken English.

Lispington explained why he had come. The dentist listened carefully.

'The mouth wide, if you please. Widest.'

'That's not necessary,' said Lispington.

'Not necessary? How can you mean, sir?'

'The tooth is in my pocket, not in my mouth,' explained Lispington. 'Here you are.'

Dr Xambis took the tooth, his eyes shining with greed.

'Beautiful! Beautiful! Very fine indeed,' he said caressingly. 'I can make the tooth in place while you sit. But first I must see this one in my mike-and-scope.'

'*Microscope*, not mike-and-scope, you fool,' the nurse hissed through her mask.

Dr Xambis and the nurse disappeared into an adjoining room. Lispington rubbed his hands. Everything was going according to plan.

Dr Xambis returned. 'Now we shall go to work at once, and fix the tooth fast, in your head, my good sir.'

He turned to the nurse, and together they mixed up what must have been at least two pounds of mortar.

'There—now I fix it fast!' he said at last.

'You have such big hands, Dr Xambis!' groaned Lispington.

'Not at all, my good sir—it is you English people who have such a small mouth!' answered Dr Xambis, pressing the tooth into position.

'Are you sure you haven't put it in upside down?' asked Lispington anxiously.

'Upside down? What is it that you are saying to me, sir? Let me look!' he exclaimed. 'Ah—yes—verily! You speak

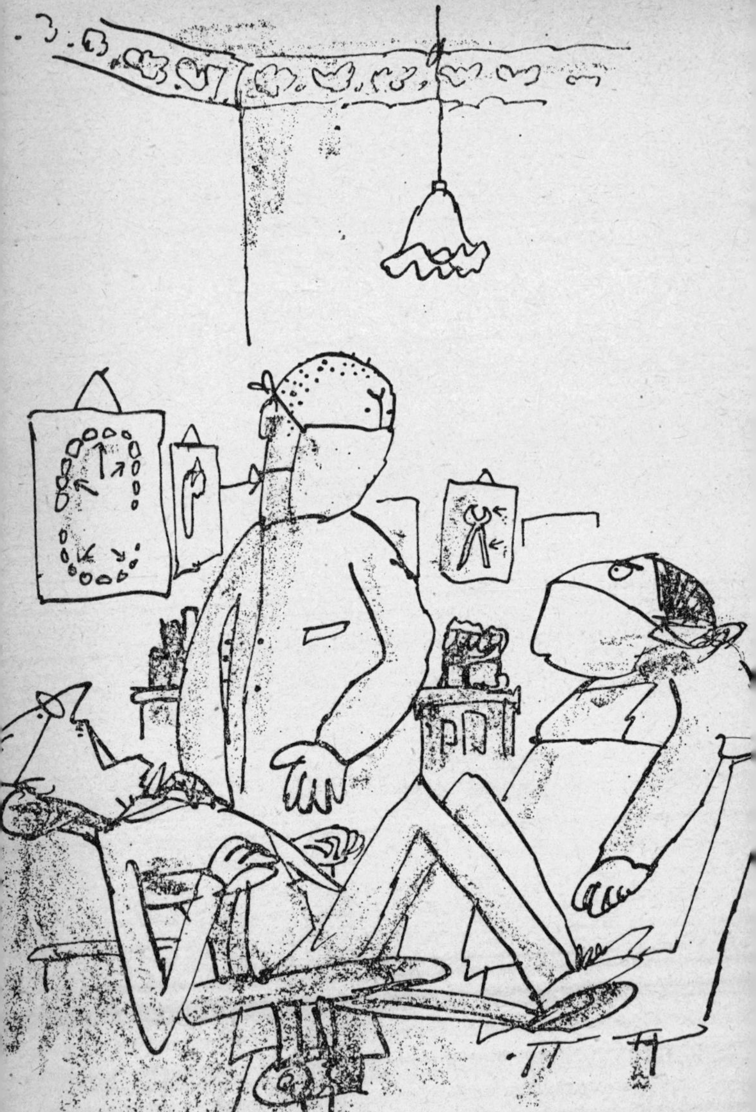

in the truth, sir! The tooth is upside down. Excuse myself! You see, it was my nurse who with fault held the mirror upside down when I fastened the tooth.'

The nurse looked daggers at Dr Xambis, but he took no notice, just wrenched out the tooth and attempted to replace it correctly.

'It is always a difficult business with these provincial arrangements,' he muttered apologetically.

'*Provisional*, not provincial, you fool,' the nurse hissed again.

'That's it!' said Dr Xambis triumphantly. 'It is fastened fast again. Now you can crack a cooky-nut with that tooth. A good joke, eh?'

'*Coconut*, you clumsy oaf!' the nurse muttered.

Lispington paid the dentist and hurried away.

Meanwhile, Agaton Sax had gone on another expedition to the castle, where he made certain valuable observations. A couple of hours later he started back to his hotel.

As he was crossing the market place, he heard excited voices and saw a big crowd outside a café. Instinctively suspecting that something dangerous was about to happen, or had just happened, he approached the crowd cautiously. There were tourists from many countries, but the majority were Greeks, engaged in a heated discussion. Agaton Sax strained his ears so as to find out the cause of the argument.

'He has no one to blame but himself!'

'That's not fair. He ought to be content with what he's got.'

'What he's got? Would *you* be content with raw fish and nothing but raw fish all day long?'

'I saw it myself! He tried to hit him! That was a rotten thing to do!'

'You are wrong, madam. Alcibiades started the whole thing.'

'That's right! I saw it. He pinched a cuttlefish from Mrs Kanneloupolous!'

'He didn't! She isn't here today, anyway.'

'Look out! He's opening his mouth!'

'Watch out! He'll bite you!'

'He's flapping his wings!'

'What lingo is he talking?'

'He's always so well-mannered. That stupid fellow must have provoked him!'

With his usual extraordinary skills in understanding an impossibly baffling situation, Agaton Sax realized that when people were shouting 'he' and 'him', they were referring to two different people. But who on earth could the 'he' be who flapped his wings, ate raw fish, and bit the other 'he'? It must be . . . Yes. that was it, it was a gigantic bird, a pelican, involved in a passionate argument with a man.

The man was Inspector Lispington.

Agaton Sax was greatly alarmed as he witnessed this scene. When you are abroad on a secret mission, you have to take great care not to get at loggerheads with—well, pelicans—for example, since a quarrel of this kind always causes a sensation, and can even produce a scandal, thus jeopardizing the whole enterprise. As soon as he had satisfied himself that neither Herr Gustaffson nor any of his gang was present, Agaton Sax forced his way through the crowd, and shouted at Lispington, 'There's an important telegram for you at your hotel, sir!' Lispington was very angry. His cheeks were flushed with rage and he bellowed at Agaton Sax (whom he did not recognize).

'This is much more important than any telegram.'

'What's going on?' said Agaton Sax, who had now come right up to him.

'This insolent pelican, who seems to be running wild in

the streets of Rhodes, has just stolen a particularly valuable parcel from me.'

'Stolen?'

'Yes! Stolen! I was walking along minding my own business, when this disreputable bird suddenly emerged from a side street. I was carrying a small parcel containing a valuable ring I had just bought and, would you believe it, that bird snatched the parcel out of my hand? He's got it stuffed away in that great mouth of his, and refuses to give it back.'

'But Lispington, you can't stand here quarrelling with a pelican, especially as you don't seem to know who he is. This is Alcibiades, and he's a very popular character here in Rhodes. He walks about the streets, and everybody enjoys feeding him and having a chat with him. He must have thought that your parcel was meant for him! Come back to the hotel with me, the telegram I told you about really is extremely important.'

Lispington made a last effort to remove his parcel from Alcibiades' mouth—but in vain! Alcibiades haughtily averted his head, refusing to co-operate. Then he stalked away, paying no further attention to Lispington or his problems.

'There isn't a telegram at the hotel,' whispered Agaton Sax as they hurried away from the scene of Lispington's defeat to the seclusion of their hotel.

'Nor is there a parcel with a ring in it,' said Lispington testily.

'No? Then why were you quarrelling with Alcibiades?'

'Because there was a parcel, only it didn't have a ring in it. It was only a small package, but it contained evidence of considerable value. And now it's in that insolent bird's maw.'

'What kind of evidence?' asked Agaton Sax, showing some concern.

'A small magnetic tape.'

'A recording you made?'

'Yes. Yesterday, I bought a miniature tape-recorder which cost me £25·50—I managed to get 5p knocked off the price. In the evening, I had dinner at an open-air restaurant. At the table next to mine there were three men, speaking a very strange language. It had no resemblance to any language that I have ever heard. Now and then, they glanced furtively at me, lowering their voices to a whisper. I decided at once that the situation called for action, so I placed my little microphone in the bread-basket, and recorded their conversation. Now that ridiculous bird has gobbled up all they said. It's a good thing I found time last night to write down everything I heard.'

'You wrote it down?'

'Yes! I played back the tape in my hotel room, and took down every word—well, as best I could, for as I told you, it's a damned odd language.'

'But this is superb. Lispington! Really, you are a fine detective.'

'That's true,' said Lispington. 'But unfortunately I'm not so good at languages. I thought perhaps you, with your remarkable flair for them, might understand, if I read it to you, what the men had been saying.'

'I'm sure I would. Have you got the notes you made?'

Lispington opened his leather briefcase and fished out a large sheet of paper. Putting on his spectacles, he said: 'You'll have to excuse my pronunciation.'

Agaton Sax sat back in his chair, closed his eyes and said only, 'I'm ready.'

Lispington cleared his throat.

'This is how it sounded to me: *D'antek lookvarklen sawknarciut fstorer. Hanaddett grernt summitsharpom maarghen, ossoansn there slookattma veeda brattn or . . .*'

'Stop!' said Agaton Sax, raising his hand. 'It's impossible!'

'Impossible?' exclaimed Lispington, lowering the paper on to his lap. 'How can you say that? I heard it myself.'

'But I don't recognize this language!' said Agaton Sax.

'Here,' Lispington offered Agaton Sax the sheet of paper in his hand. 'If you don't believe me, see for yourself. This is what I wrote down.'

Agaton Sax took the paper and read the words written on it.

'Did you play the tape several times?' he asked.

'Yes, at least ten times. I wanted to be sure that when I wrote it down I got it right. It could be used as evidence in a court of law, you know!'

'Hmmm . . . 'Agaton Sax pulled gently at his moustache.

'You're an expert in Graelic, aren't you, Mr Sax? Could it be a Graelic dialect?'

'No!'

'Bulgarian then? Or Crillic? Or some forgotten Transsylvanian dialect?'

'No!'

'What about Mesopotamian? Or Gordian?'

'Gordian? There is no such language!' exclaimed Agaton Sax. He was beginning to lose his temper.

'Well Mesmerian? Briscian? Fiddleonian?'

'No!'

'What about Mixteronian—West Ipswichian—Lemonadian?'

'Mixteronian, Lemonadian! You know perfectly well that there are no such languages! I could add to the list of non-existent languages, too, if you like. What about Mastodonian, Chiropodian, and Atlantian. Or perhaps you would prefer Cholerian or Melancholian. No one's ever spoken them either,' he muttered.

'What's that you're mumbling about?' said Lispington tartly. 'Shall I read you some more?' he added, as Agaton Sax began to walk backwards and forwards across the room.

'No, thank you. I'll read it to myself again.'

And he went on with his silent reading, puffing at an enormous cigar and sending heavy clouds of smoke up to the ceiling.

'Well?' said Lispington sarcastically after a few minutes. 'Have you got it?'

Agaton Sax did not answer, because he hadn't heard the question. He was getting really worried; failure to read Lispington's notes could be disastrous.

It was a quarter of an hour before he spoke again. 'Lispington,' he said, 'this is impossible. Are you certain that . . . I mean, had you . . . were you . . . Well, let's put it this way. You had been forced to take a hadromyscofilogenatriumdormatolinfilosofin pill, hadn't you? Are you *quite* sure that you weren't a little bit . . . how shall I put it . . . well : you don't think you dreamt the whole thing, do you?'

'Dreamt it!' Lispington was horrified. 'I never dream! Certainly not when I'm working. Never!'

Five minutes later Agaton Sax had almost disappeared behind the smoke cloud from his cigar.

'Are you there, Mr Sax?'

No answer.

'Are you still there?' Lispington repeated.

'Who do you want?'

'You! Are you there?'

'Am I?'

'Are you, or aren't you?'

But Agaton Sax wasn't listening. With a hand that shook from the strain of the past half hour, he checked off the words on the paper with a pencil, trying to verify a theory which was so outrageous when it first came to him that he could hardly believe it. It needed all his concentration, and he had no time for Lispington's interruptions.

Five minutes later he was sure that his theory was right.

He stood up triumphantly.

'I've got it!'

'You know the language?' asked Lispington. 'What is it, Catastrophian?'

'I'll tell you later,' said Agaton Sax airily. 'First, let me read you an English translation of the text. It goes like this: "You can't imagine how ridiculous the chap looked! He was wearing a green velvet belt and a broad-brimmed slouch-hat . . . Did you say a green belt? It must be him! Who? The one over there—can't you see him? Look he's sliding rather furtively through the doorway near the shoe-maker's shop. Can you see, there's a whole lot of them all jostling to get through that narrow doorway? Look at their faces. They must be crooks of some kind . . ." '

'This is absurd!' interrupted Lispington. 'What on earth does it mean?'

'It means that the three mysterious strangers sitting at the table next to yours were not mysterious at all. They were just ordinary tourists. One of them told the others that he had seen a ridiculous looking fellow wearing a a green belt. As he was speaking one of his friends spotted the man, with several companions. To their astonishment they saw that all the men were trying to hide their faces. Do you know what, Lispington?'

'No!'

'I'll tell you: I am absolutely sure that the men your mysterious strangers saw were Herr Gustaffson and his gang.'

'Outrageous!' exclaimed Lispington.

'But true,' said Agaton Sax calmly. 'And together—you with your eye for suspicious behaviour, and I with my knowledge of languages—we have succeeded in tracking down and identifying Herr Gustaffson and his gang.'

'But the language! What language were they speaking?'

'Swedish,' answered Agaton Sax. 'One of the most difficult languages in the world. It took me four years to learn it.'

8

Happy Families and high stakes

'Swedish?' said Lispington suspiciously.

'Yes. Nothing could be more likely. Rhodes is full of Swedish tourists. You happened to sit near three of them, and they happened to see Herr Gustaffson and his gang. Now, tell me exactly when you recorded the conversation.'

'Thirteen-and-a-half hours ago.'

'Good. Are you ready?'

'Yes. What for?'

'For an important expedition. We'll leave immediately. Do you remember precisely where you were sitting in the restaurant?'

'Of course! I always draw maps of places I visit and plans of restaurants I eat in. Here's a diagram I made. There's my own table, complete with salt-cellar, pepper-pot, and bread-basket. The microphone was hidden in the basket. The salt-cellar was wooden, the bread-basket woven with some sort of rushes. And there's the table where the three Swedes were sitting. There were five chairs at the table, two of them were empty, and one had a broken back —that one there, in the left-hand corner of the diagram.'

'I see,' said Agaton Sax patiently.

'Please don't interrupt, you break my chain of thought. That's the door into the restaurant's kitchen, it was painted green, rather stained and battered. The owner of the restaurant sat on a bar stool near the door smoking a cigar—no, wait a minute, it can't have been the owner himself, it must have been his brother, the one who used to work at the harbour but has now retired. He seems to like sitting at . . . '

'Yes, yes, that's fine, but what street was it in?'

'What street?'

'Yes! What street was the restaurant in?'

'I don't know.'

'You don't know? You have a detailed map of the restaurant, but you don't know where it was?'

'But I didn't draw a map of the town! You buy those in a shop, there's no need to make them, is there?'

'No, I don't suppose there is.'

'Wait a minute. I think I can remember. There was a big poster on the wall, I couldn't understand what it said.'

'Perhaps it was in Modern Greek.'

'Oh no, far more difficult. Actually I wrote it down,' he added, handing Agaton Sax a scrap of paper.

'But this is Swedish again! It says: *Come and enjoy Swedish meat balls. As good as the ones your mother used to make. Welcome to Sweden in Rhodes*. I know the place. Come on, there's not a moment to lose.'

They dashed off, Tickie at their heels, and in no time at all found the restaurant serving Swedish food.

'Look!' said Lispington. 'There's the shoe-maker's shop. You see the doorway beside it? That's where they went in.'

'We must be very careful!' murmured Agaton Sax. 'Herr Gustaffson has eyes in the back of his head.'

He looked carefully up and down the street, but saw nothing at all suspicious anywhere.

'The coast's clear,' he whispered. 'Let's walk slowly towards the house Herr Gustaffson and his gang went into.'

On the wall of the house there was a notice bearing the

one word HOTEL. The hotel seemed to be on the first floor. Everything looked peaceful and innocent and there was nothing to show that Herr Gustaffson might be living there. But suddenly Agaton Sax tugged Lispington's right sleeve.

'Someone's coming!'

He was right. A man who appeared to be in a great hurry came out of the door. He was out of breath and looked as if he had been running up and down more stairs than the house had storeys.

'That must be Moscow Jim,' whispered Agaton Sax.

'Moscow Jim? In Rhodes?'

'Yes. He is one of Herr Gustaffson's most trusted accomplices. We'd better follow him.'

At that moment, Tickie rushed off in pursuit of the man. Agaton Sax let her catch up with him. When he saw her he stopped and growled, 'Get off, you dirty beast. Go on, get off!'

Agaton Sax blew one blast on the special whistle he always carried. It was pitched so high that it could only be heard by animals. Tickie came to heel as soon as she heard it, and Moscow Jim disappeared round the corner.

'He'll get away!' gasped Lispington. 'We must go after him!'

'No, not now! He might spot us. We'll let him get a good start.'

He bent down and patted Tickie on the head.

'Good dog,' he said. 'Follow that scent!'

He put Tickie on the lead, and she set off eagerly following the scent of the vanished Moscow Jim. Tickie led them down a narrow lane, and stopped outside a broken-down door, which had evidently just been opened and closed again by someone inside. The house was old and miserably kept and at first sight seemed to have been built into a thick stone wall, part of which could be seen at the back of the house. However, when they got close enough to examine it properly, Lispington and Agaton Sax discovered there was a narrow passage between the house and the wall. Once in the passage they noticed a small window in the side wall of the house. It was broken and peering through they saw it led into a dark corridor. They looked at each other, nodded, and climbed swiftly through, dropping noiselessly on to the floor inside.

They could hear a faint murmur of voices somewhere

in the darkness and tiptoed along the corridor, followed by Tickie.

'There!' whispered Agaton Sax, pointing into the darkness. A feeble streak of light shone through a small hole in the wall. They moved silently towards it.

'There?' whispered Lispington. 'Do you think that . . . ?'

'Yes!'

'What shall we do? Arrest them?'

'Not yet. I'll use my walkie-talkie first.'

'Why?'

'It's always useful.'

'All right.'

They pressed themselves against the wall. Agaton Sax fixed up his walkie-talkie, which, though tiny, was equipped with transmitter, microphone, and receiver. Now they could hear the voices quite clearly and distinguish every word easily.

Agaton Sax peered through the hole in the wall.

'Can you see them?' whispered Lispington.

'Yes! The whole lot are there. Herr Gustaffson, his gang, and the Colossus!'

'The Colossus?'

'Yes, it must be.'

'How do you know it's him?'

'It must be. See for yourself.'

Agaton Sax stood back and Lispington bent down and looked through the hole.

'This is a bad angle for me. It hurts my back,' he said peevishly. 'Isn't there another chink somewhere?'

'Down there, just above the floor. You'll have to lie down.'

Lispington did so. Now they could both see the room, which was absolutely empty of furniture, except for a simple wooden table and a few chairs. On the table were a couple of paraffin lamps, a bottle of mineral water, and some glasses. Along one side of the table sat Herr Gustaffson and four of his accomplices, among them Moscow Jim, who had just come in. On the other side sat just one man, an enormous fellow whose face was almost entirely covered by a black mask. There was no doubt that this was the mysterious Colossus of Rhodes. Equally certain was the fact that Agaton Sax and Lispington were looking in on a top-level underworld conference.

'Now that my deputy director, Mr Moscow Jim, has joined us, perhaps it would be in order to declare the conference open?' said Herr Gustaffson. He was in a good mood, but even when he made a joke his voice had a sinister note in it.

'Of course!' bellowed the Colossus.

'Pray keep your voice down,' said Herr Gustaffson blandly. 'They might hear you at the police station.'

'Sure, I'll do my best,' said the Colossus amiably, lowering his voice.

'Good!' said Herr Gustaffson. 'Let me outline the situation. As I understand it, you have invited us to join you in a big-scale project. You know where the Colossus of Rhodes lies buried and you need some strong, intelligent men to help you dig it out. Is that right?'

'Corright,' answered the Colossus.

'What did you say?' said Herr Gustaffson frowning slightly.

That's corright—that's right, correct, I think I mean.'

'Never mind what you mean, as long as you know what you are talking about. You say we can make a fortune out of this old ruin. What makes you think that and how could we do it?'

'Because the stratue is bronzed, with much of gold in it. It's the most exprensive stratue in the world. It's worth a million pounds, at least a million pounds.'

'So far, so good,' said Herr Gustaffson. 'And you have a map of the place where the stra . . . statue is buried?'

'Sure I have. Here!' And the Colossus patted his inside pocket.

'May I see the map?' said Herr Gustaffson.

'Of course. As soon as we have talked money between us. Sixty per cent for me, and forty for you.'

'Impossible!' said Herr Gustaffson coldly. 'There are five of us, remember, and only one of you.'

'He who is alone, is strong, as we say in Rhodes.'

'But five are stronger,' said Herr Gustaffson.

'I have the map,' thundered the Colossus.

'I'm sorry,' said Herr Gustaffson, standing up, 'but my company would never agree to such terms. The shareholders would be furious.'

'You have not the only chair-holders!' said the Colossus, a note of menace creeping into his voice.

Herr Gustaffson frowned again.

'Fifty per cent for you, fifty for us,' he said.

'Impossible!' thundered the Colossus. 'I have more taxes to pay than you, Herr Gustaffson! Here you can see my tax returns for last year!'

He produced a greasy paper, and held it up to the light of the paraffin lamp.

'Don't talk to me about taxes!' shouted Herr Gustaffson angrily. 'We pay far more taxes in England than you do in Rhodes, I know that because I have read the reports of the International Committee for the Study of World Taxation Systems. Here's my tax demand for last year. Just take a look at that.'

And Herr Gustaffson, too, drew a paper from his pocket. It was crumpled and stained—evidently with the tears he had shed over it as he filled it in.

'Bah! A fool's civication!' jeered the Colossus.

'A falsification!' raged Herr Gustaffson. 'Are you mad? Have you ever heard of anyone falsifying his own tax-demand in order to pay *more* money to the tax-collector?'

'This is absurd,' whispered Lispington.

The Colossus leant back in his chair, and stared at Herr Gustaffson through the slits in his black mask.

'There is only one way of settling this con-flicks,' he thundered.

'And what is that?' said Herr Gustaffson, on his guard against treachery.

'The cards shall decide,' said the Colossus. 'We'll play cards. If you win, we share equal. If I win, I take sixty per cent, and you forty.'

'It's a deal,' said Herr Gustaffson without hesitation. 'What would you like to play, contract bridge?'

'Beggar-my-neighbour,' announced the Colossus at once.

'Impossible!' declared Herr Gustaffson. 'That's a child's game. I haven't played it for years. What about canasta? Or poker?'

'Happy Families,' thundered the Colossus.

'Happy Families?' exclaimed Herr Gustaffson, so astonished that he gave in. 'Have you a pack of Happy Family cards with you?'

'Yes,' said the Colossus, producing a pack of cards from one of his inside pockets.

'May I check the cards?' said Herr Gustaffson innocently. 'Just to check that the pack is complete?'

'Sure! Go ahead. Double check whatever you like.'

With an experienced hand, Herr Gustaffson counted and shuffled the cards.

'Whose deal is it? Mine?' he said.

'Sure!' said the Colossus.

Herr Gustaffson dealt the cards. He and The Colossus

picked up their hands and stared suspiciously at each other. As everybody knows, a Happy Families pack is not made up of the usual four suits, hearts, diamonds, clubs, spades, but of a number of families consisting of mother, father, son and daughter. For example, there's Mr Bung the Brewer, his wife Mrs Bung, son Master Bung and daughter Miss Bung; Mr Tape the tailor, Mr Pots the painter, Mr Soot the chimney sweep and so on, all complete with their families. The object of the game is to complete more families than your opponent by asking, in turn, for cards. If your opponent has the card you ask for he must give it to you, and you have the right to ask again. If he hasn't got the card you want, then the turn passes to him.

The consequences of the game that followed (watched by Agaton Sax and Lispington) affected the future of the whole criminal world. We describe it in detail here, so as to show you just how shrewd and callous top criminals can be when they are dealing with their rivals.

The Colossus had the first turn and asked Herr Gustaffson for Miss Pots the painter's daughter. He already had Mr Pots, Mrs Pots and Master Pots, so when Herr Gustaffson reluctantly handed over the card, that completed his first family.

Herr Gustaffson was absolutely certain that he would win the game. He was a masterly card player. But this time he could do nothing right. Time and again he asked for the very card the Colossus hadn't got, and had to forfeit his turn. He wanted Mr Bun the baker and Mrs Grits the grocer's wife in order to complete these two families—but he was never lucky.

After three minutes, the Colossus had the Pots, the Bones, the Dips and the Chips. Herr Gustaffson had nothing. He turned and looked suspiciously at the wall behind him. Was there a mirror hidden there in which the Colossus could see his cards? No, there was no mirror, nor could he see anything else that the Colossus might be using, either on the wall or the table.

Agaton Sax was listening intently to his little receiver. Things were happening just as he had expected they would. The Colossus asked for yet another card from Herr Gustaffson. 'That completes the Bungs!' he roared happily, displaying the four members of the brewery family.

Herr Gustaffson was still managing to keep a hold on his temper, though the strain was beginning to show. For in his super-charged brain various notions and fleeting ideas were chasing each other like flashes of summer lightning. How could this be? How could this colossal half-wit beat *him*, the possessor of one of the sharpest intelligences in the business of crime?

A moment later the Colossus had won. Herr Gustaffson found himself without a single family to his credit. The Colossus leant back in his chair, and beamed complacently at his opponent.

'I can't believe it,' said Herr Gustaffson, ashen-faced. 'I have met many card sharpers in my time. Men who think nothing of cheating at bridge, canasta, poker or vingt-et-un. But never before have I met a man so mean, so treacherous, so base, as to cheat when playing Happy Families! You are a disgrace to our profession, Mr Colossus, an unscrupulous contemptible adventurer. I am heartily sorry that I ever entered into partnership with such a crook!'

'That's right! We've had enough of your swindles!' roared Moscow Jim, leaping up so violently that he pushed over his chair.

'Precisely,' said Herr Gustaffson, laying the three members of the Bun family he had managed to acquire down on the table.

'What are you talking about?' thundered the Colossus, pushing over a chair in his turn.

'About your cheating at cards, sir!'

The Colossus turned pale beneath his black mask.

'You must be mad!' he raged.

'Oh, no I'm not,' replied Herr Gustaffson icily. 'You have been marking the cards all the time we were playing.

Look here! Look at this thumb print on the back of Master Grits the grocer's son.'

'That's your own mark, you humbug!' said the Colossus, pounding the table with his enormous fists.

'It is not, sir!' said Herr Gustaffson. 'I can't do business with a man like you! Give me that map!'

'The map? Are you absolutely out of your mind?' exploded the Colossus. 'This is *my* map! Are you a common thief, Herr Gustaffson?'

'Yes,' said Herr Gustaffson, 'I am. And I would like to draw your attention to the fact that you are surrounded by five exceptionally strong men. The game is up, I'm afraid. Please hand me the map.'

'He's got a nerve, I must admit,' whispered Lispington admiringly.

For a moment it looked as if the Colossus would refuse to give in. But then he hesitated, as if he were listening to an inner voice advising him to play for safety. He threw the map on the table.

'Your health!' said Herr Gustaffson, picking his glass up from the table.

Enraged, the Colossus raised his glass and emptied it at a gulp. Half a minute later he was fast asleep. Herr Gustaffson had doctored the contents with one of his potent sleeping pills.

'Now we're in trouble!' whispered Lispington. 'What will happen next?'

9

Lispington hangs on

The answer to Lispington's question came immediately.

Herr Gustaffson's five assistants lifted up the Colossus and carried him outside to a car parked in the lane. Agaton Sax and Lispington followed cautiously. Fortunately the crooks drove only a few yards, then stopped and carried the Colossus through a door barely wide enough for them all to squeeze through.

'We mustn't follow for a moment,' whispered Agaton Sax, restraining Lispington who was eager to rush straight in. 'In a few minutes, Herr Gustaffson and his men will come out. When they do, you shadow them. I'll sneak into the house and keep watch over the Colossus. O.K.?'

'O.K.'

Lispington hailed a taxi. As soon as the crooks appeared he whispered to the driver: 'Scotland Yard. Follow that car.'

Agaton Sax approached the house very cautiously. As he had expected, he caught a glimpse of a shady-looking individual edging his way round the house and sneaking in through a back-door.

He was in a tight spot. If this unknown character spotted him anything might happen. Agaton Sax was fully aware of the risk, but he decided, without hesitation, to take it. He went in.

Meanwhile, Lispington's taxi had been unsuccessful in trailing the gang's car. The chase had covered the greater part of the town when suddenly the car disappeared—apparently vanishing into thin air.

'Damn,' murmured Lispington. He paid off the driver and hurried back to his hotel, where he waited impatiently for Agaton Sax, who arrived half an hour later. He listened in silence to Lispington's sad tale.

'Which way were they going when you lost them?' he asked.

'South,' said Lispington.

They stowed Clever Dick and Lispington's P.C.M. into the boot of the car Agaton Sax had hired, and drove slowly south through the streets of Rhodes, all the time keeping a look-out for Herr Gustaffson and his gang. After a while they passed beyond the city limits. Dusk was falling as they drove up into the hills, seeing the lights of the city fade into the distance behind them. No clues, not a footprint or a fingerprint! Nothing. Where was Herr Gustaffson, and what cunning move was he—at that very moment perhaps—preparing?

'We'd better consult Clever Dick,' said Agaton Sax abruptly, stopping the car on the brow of a hill.

'Clever Dick?' asked Lispington, displeased at this sudden interruption of their journey. 'How can he help?'

'He can answer a lot of questions.'

'I'll bring my P.C.M. along, too,' said Lispington. 'Just to make sure,' he added obscurely. He picked up the small black box and tucked it lovingly under one arm before getting out of the car. It took all their strength to lift Clever Dick's two halves out of the boot. There was an awful moment when Agaton Sax tripped on a stone and dropped his half. It rolled away from him and landed in a ditch a few yards further off. With Lispington's help he managed to haul it on to the road again, and re-assembled it as quickly as he could.

'We'd better check that he's come to no harm before we start asking him questions,' he said, pressing a couple of buttons. There was a faint buzzing sound and Clever Dick announced:

'$2 \times 2 = 3{\cdot}99999999999$.'

'That's not right!' exclaimed Lispington. '$2 \times 2 = 4$, any fool knows that.'

'No doubt,' replied Agaton Sax drily, 'But you must admit it would be hard to get nearer to the right answer than Clever Dick did. Just a second—I'll oil him.'

He squirted some of Aunt Matilda's sewing-machine oil into a hole in the computer, then pressed a few more buttons.

'$3 \times 3 = 8{\cdot}9999999999999$,' answered Clever Dick.

'What a masterly miss!' exclaimed Lispington.

'Don't be too hasty! He's probably suffering from shock, and as a result had a minor concussion of his numerical system. Nothing more than a temporary disorder.' Agaton Sax pressed one button after another. Big ones, small ones, red, green and blue ones. Then he pulled several small levers.

'Now what are you doing?' asked Lispington impatiently.

'I'm feeding him.'

'Feeding him?'

'Yes, I tell him what I know. Then he'll tell me what we ought to do.'

Lispington shook his head. But in spite of himself he eyed Clever Dick with a certain amount of respect.

'You mean you tell him *all* you know?'

'Almost all.'

'About my tooth?'

'Yes. And the dentist. And the dentist's nurse.'

'I see.'

Clever Dick seemed to be ready with his answer. It was delivered on a strip of ticker tape, which Agaton Sax tore off quickly. He read out the following words: *Oye Rext bu yn oyem geimd igianxt tlu nemxu! Tlu fhuinum as dingumyex phex.*

'Good Heavens, man, what's that meant to mean?' exclaimed Lispington. 'It must be stark, raving Swedish! I'd better destroy the paper at once.'

He tore the slip of paper from Agaton Sax's hand, and gave it to his P.C.M., which gobbled it up in one greedy gulp. Agaton Sax was so absorbed by the problem the message had set him that he never even noticed his colleague's rash gesture. He fed another short question to Clever Dick and had his answer within seconds: *Tlu Fyhyxxex yc Mlydux nyt-dingumyex bet tlu nemxu dingumyex phex.*

'Preposterous!' shouted Lispington, tearing off the strip of paper. 'Clever Dick is raving mad.'

And he fed his own machine with the strange message.

'Don't do that,' said Agaton Sax. Beads of sweat had appeared on his forehead. 'There's more to come.'

Clever Dick was trembling with the effort of getting out his answers so speedily.

Tlu fhuinum tlu fhuinum Bu yn oyem geimd igianxt tlu fhuinum! A, Fhuvum Dafk, wimn oye!

'This is Double Dutch!' exclaimed Lispington. 'We have no time to spare for this sort of madness! Come on, we must get back to town! *Fhuvum Dafk!* I haven't heard anything so stupid since I was appointed Chief Inspector!'

'Just a minute, I know what's wrong,' Agaton Sax implored. 'There's a slight fault in Clever Dick's letter-arranging mechanism, what could be called an alphabetical breakdown. Certain letters are mixed up. *S* becomes *x*, *a* becomes *i*, *h* becomes *l*, *e* becomes *u*, *c* becomes *f*, *m* becomes *r*, *o* becomes *y*—and vice versa! Once you've realized that it's quite simple. Roughly translated, what *Fhuvum Dafk*—sorry—Clever Dick, is trying to say is this: *You must be on your guard against the nurse! The cleaner is dangerous plus. The Colossus of Rhodes not dangerous but the nurse dangerous plus. The cleaner! The cleaner! Be on your guard against the cleaner! I, Clever Dick, warn you!*'

'The cleaner?' Lispington was in despair.

'That's right. The cleaner who let you out after Herr Gustaffson had given you the sleeping pill and locked you up. Everything will be explained in due course. I know now exactly what has happened—and why. All we have to do is . . . Look at that car!'

He pointed to a car which flashed past at terrific speed heading into the city.

'Herr Gustaffson!' exclaimed Lispington. 'At last! We've found him!'

He was not mistaken about the identity of the men in the car: they were Herr Gustaffson and his four assistants. Fortunately they did not notice the two detectives standing by the side of the road.

'We'll get them this time,' said Agaton Sax grimly, as they packed their machines away in the back of the car and set off in pursuit of the crooks.

The other car turned into a small lane on the outskirts of the town. Agaton Sax and Lispington watched Herr Gustaffson and his men leap out and run across to one of the entrances to the old castle.

'They're going straight to the spot I marked with an X on the forged map,' whispered Agaton Sax, rubbing his hands in triumph. 'They think the statue of the ancient Colossus lies buried there. Just what I wanted them to think.'

'This is marvellous,' said Lispington, as pleased as his friend. 'I've got the real map in my pocket.'

'Do you mind giving it to me?' said Agaton Sax.

'If you like,' said Lispington generously.

They followed the crooks, keeping their distance and moving with great caution. The thieves made their way stealthily up a winding staircase. It was pitch dark, and the silence was broken only by occasional grunts from the gang—grunts which were instantly hushed by Herr Gustaffson.

There was now not a sound to be heard. The two detectives stopped in their tracks and listened anxiously.

'We're in great danger,' murmured Agaton Sax, 'but we must go on.'

'Shouldn't we alert the Rhodes police?' asked Lispington.

'Never!'

As they moved slowly upwards, they saw a faint light glimmering in the darkness above them.

'The stars,' whispered Agaton Sax. Hc pressed on up the stairs until he came out on to the roof, bending to give Lispington a helping hand with the final step. Far below them in the street they could hear the roar of the traffic, but no sound of any kind gave a clue to where the thieves were hiding on the roof.

Suddenly a slim shaft of light from a torch pierced the darkness. Instinctively Agaton Sax and Lispington flung themselves to the floor, in time to see two figures emerge from the darkness in a far corner of the great roof.

There was no time for them to escape down the stairs. 'Over here,' whispered Agaton Sax, tugging Lispington's sleeve.

Just where they were standing, were two thick ropes, fastened securely to rings in the stonework. They had been left by workmen who had been working up there all day repairing the parapet.

'Climb over the edge and let yourself down the other side,' whispered Agaton Sax, 'then hang on until they have gone. Press yourself as close up to the wall as you can.'

Showing surprising agility they climbed over the parapet and slid some ten yards down the rope. Keeping an ear open for any shout that would warn them the crooks had spotted them. It came. They heard a harsh whisper: 'Rubbish! I can't see anyone.'

'I swear I saw someone,' came the answer, urgent and scared.

'You are a bunch of incompetent half-wits, every rotten one of you.' The voice, coldly impatient, could only belong to Herr Gustaffson. 'Get a move on. We must go.'

Agaton Sax and Lispington heard them leave the roof, and knew it was time for them to climb back on to the roof if they were to keep track of the gang. But going up proved much more difficult than going down.

'Are you ready, Lispington?' said Agaton Sax.

'I'm ready, but I can't do it,' gasped Lispington, trying in vain to climb up the rope, which seemed to take offence at his efforts and do all it could to thwart them.

'Try to get a purchase with your foot against the wall. Like this.'

Lispington tried.

'My legs are too long,' he moaned. 'They push my body too far away from the wall.'

'I see.'

Agaton Sax tried to think of a way out of this embarrassing situation. Climbing up a rope was child's play to him, but he was anxious not to say so, for fear of hurting Lispington's feelings.

'Can you hang on?' he asked.

'Yes, I'm fine.'

'You're sure you don't feel down-hearted?'

'Down-hearted! On the contrary, my spirits are up even if my legs are down.'

'What shall we do?'

'We'll have to wait.'

'Wait? What for?'

'Until the crooks have gone.'

'We could try. But won't your arms get stiff, Lispington?'

'Oh no, I'll do some exercises. This sort of thing.' And Lispington showed his colleague how to keep your arm muscles from stiffening when hanging from a rope some twenty metres above the ground. Considering that even a slight mistake might be fatal, Agaton Sax had to admire his colleague's remarkable courage.

'The best thing would be for me to climb up first, and then hoist him up after me,' he thought. 'But then he'd never let me, he's far too proud.'

'Mr Sax,' said Lispington suddenly.

'Yes?'

'Do you remember that conversation we had over the phone just before I was . . . just before Herr Gustaffson attacked me in my office?'

'Of course I remember it.'

'Do you also remember that I mentioned an order I expected to have conferred on me?'

'I remember that, too.'

'Do you know, Mr Sax, last year I hoped that I might get a W.H.I.S.K. Second class.'

'Well?'

'Well, I didn't get it, that's all.'

'You didn't get it? Well, I never . . . '

'It surprises you, doesn't it Mr Sax? It was the cashier who put a stop to it. What a wicked man! He was jealous of me. He hadn't got an order himself, and he couldn't bear the thought of my having one.'

'People can be like that. He sounds a very disagreeable person, I must say.'

'I suppose in a small country like Sweden, your orders must be pretty small, mustn't they, Mr Sax?'

'Oh yes, unfortunately they are,' said Agaton Sax. 'Far too small. I am also disappointed and upset, for I, too, have suffered from the jealousy of colleagues. But then I have received honours from overseas far greater than the Swedish ones. Would you like to be given a Swedish order, Mr Lispington?'

'I would indeed! It would hang perfectly here. *Here* I mean,' he added, letting go the rope with his right hand and pointing to the left side of his breast. Agaton Sax turned pale.

'For heaven's sake, be careful!' he whispered.

They were silent again.

'If we fail to make an arrest, the British Government will be terribly angry with me,' said Lispington suddenly. 'They won't trust me with another important case for years.'

'We *will* make an arrest,' said Agaton Sax firmly, 'don't worry. Inspector Lispington,' he went on after a moment's pause, 'isn't it about time . . . that we . . . how shall I put it . . . that we . . . I mean, after all, we've known each other so long . . . couldn't we . . . be just a little less formal with each other?'

'Less formal, Mr Sax?'

'Yes, I mean . . . well, you know, in a dangerous situation like this one . . . it takes time to say "Inspector Lispington" —it would be quicker to say just . . . well . . . just your Christian name.'

'Oh yes, I see what you mean, Mr Sax—Agaton, that is. I agree entirely. What a good idea!'

'I'm glad you think so, my dear Joshua. Now, I have an idea. I'm going to climb back on to the roof, and then pull you up after me.'

'I can't let you go up first, Agaton. Absolutely not! Look! There's a big stone jutting out from the wall here, and if I press my foot against it . . . like this . . . I can . . . I can pull myself up . . . like this . . . '

'No, don't do it! It's dangerous!' Agaton Sax sounded terrified.

'No it's not. Look! Like this!'

Lispington pushed hard with his foot, moved his hands a few inches up the rope and hauled as hard as he could. There was a moment of suspense, and then he fell, panting with exhaustion, on to the roof.

At that moment something happened which no one could have anticipated. Agaton Sax, clinging helplessly to his rope, was silhouetted against the wall, caught in the beams of a whole battery of searchlights that had been put up in the garden below. As the lights swung on to him a voice called out something in a language that no one seemed to understand (actually it was Modern Greek). It was a female voice, strident and determined. But this was not the only voice to break the silence of the night. Another sound, equally significant, was heard—the loud barking of a dog.

'Are you there, Agaton?' whispered Lispington, leaning out over the parapet.

As he listened for an answer from Agaton Sax, Lispington heard a slight movement behind him. He leapt back. Two shadowy figures emerged from the dark and threw their arms round him. Before he could give so much as a warning shout, he was bundled up and carried off.

10

Aunt Matilda comes in at the finish

Agaton Sax stayed where he was, hanging motionless on his rope. For a few moments of almost unbearable suspense he had no idea what was going to happen—he didn't even know for certain what had just happened. But he could make a pretty good guess.

Had they seen him? Not a sound came from the roof, though from the park he could hear excited voices shouting in Greek: 'Call the fire brigade!' 'Throw a life-belt up!' 'Alert the police!'

Agaton Sax shinned up the rope and crawled over the parapet, where the first thing he noticed was Lispington's P.C.M., carelessly left behind by the crooks at the time of the kidnapping.

There was no time to lose. Agaton Sax knew where to find Herr Gustaffson and his gang, since he himself had drawn the forged map and put on the X to indicate where the statue of the ancient Colossus might be found (or rather might not be found). He crept silently across the roof, and found a stairway leading down into the interior of the castle. At the far end of a long, narrow, dark corridor he saw a pale light. It came from under a door, and Agaton Sax realized with a thrill that he must be very near the spot he had marked on the map. The thieves were within his grasp.

His heart beat faster. He was playing a dangerous game, and the stakes were high; but there was no turning back now.

He adjusted the P.C.M. so as to have it ready if he needed it. Lispington had told him that it could be used for other things if necessary, not just the one indicated by its name.

There was a crack in the wooden door and he peered through. Inside was a large room, unfurnished, and lit only by the light which came from several torches; torches that were carried by Herr Gustaffson and his men.

Against one of the walls sat Mr Lispington, perched on a gigantic cannon ball. His legs were crossed, his arms folded, and the expression on his face a mixture of pride, anger and contempt.

Towering over him stood Herr Gustaffson himself.

Agaton Sax flung open the door.

Herr Gustaffson spun round, as he heard the door open, and saw—Agaton Sax. What a shock for him! Not even in the very worst of nightmares had he dreamed that Agaton Sax might be in Rhodes.

Courage failed the thieves at the sight of their most deadly enemy. With trembling lips they cried, 'Help us! Agaton Sax has come. Help!'

Herr Gustaffson rounded on them. 'Silence, you pathetic cowards!' he ordered coldly. 'I'm in command here, not Agaton Sax!'

'I'm innocent, Mr Sax, I swear I am!' begged Finn the Forger.

'I didn't do it. You know I couldn't, don't you?' pleaded another. Agaton Sax was amused to see it was the notorious Leatherjacket Pat.

'Herr Gustaffson strong-armed me into it; I didn't want to, I swear, your lordship!' wheedled Cauliflower Charlie.

'Silence, you great boobies!'

Herr Gustaffson raised his right hand in a gesture that

indicated clearly he had heard enough. Then he turned to Agaton Sax and smiled jauntily.

'You've come at the right moment, Mr Sax. I've just discovered this map is a forgery, and no doubt you are the forger. The game is up, Mr Sax! I must ask you to give me the original map.'

Agaton Sax smiled back at him.

'It is my duty to give you a most solemn warning, Herr Gustaffson,' he said. 'No doubt you have noticed the box which I am carrying.' He paused. 'You have noticed it, haven't you?'

Herr Gustaffson saw the P.C.M. and turned slightly pale, but he did not answer.

'You have no idea what this machine is capable of, Herr Gustaffson,' he went on, 'but I can assure you that it is quite within its powers to shatter any dreams you may have about hidden statues!'

'It's the killer-ray!' panicked Finn the Forger.

'Silence,' thundered Herr Gustaffson, '*I* do the talking here!'

His words were brave, but his face was pale; he knew that Agaton Sax never made empty threats.

'Let Mr Lispington come over here—or I will switch on the machine,' ordered Agaton Sax.

Herr Gustaffson hesitated, his brain was working fast, trying to keep one move ahead of Agaton Sax.

'O.K.,' he said at last. 'You get Lispington, and I . . . '

'And you . . . ?'

'I'm free to go,' answered Herr Gustaffson, coldly calculating.

'Done,' said Agaton Sax. 'Inspector Lispington—come over here. You, Herr Gustaffson, go backwards through the door behind you!'

'Hurrah! A brilliant solution! Long live Agaton Sax!'

shouted the four accomplices, in a last desperate effort to curry favour with the arm of the law.

Herr Gustaffson nodded to Lispington, who immediately got up and went over to Agaton Sax. They shook hands Lispington. He, Herr Gustaffson, still had the fourteen odd warmly.

Herr Gustaffson, polite as always, bowed. He smiled mockingly as he turned away. Agaton Sax was welcome to million pounds he had taken from the Colossus.

But, even as he lifted his hands to open the door, it was opened from the outside. He stiffened, and stood motionless. Someone stood in the doorway, pointing a revolver at him.

Lispington gasped with astonishment.

'Tlu Fhuinum!' he cried. 'It's her! It's *tlu fhuinum*—the cleaner. It's her!'

'Exactly,' said Agaton Sax in a low voice. 'It's her all right. I was expecting her. Clever Dick was right—he had reached the same conclusion as myself: Beware of the cleaner!'

There was no mistaking her. She was a broad-shouldered, well-built woman, and she wore a belted leather coat. Her expression was forbidding and her eyes flashed fire.

Her voice was deep, and sent a thrill of fear through all who heard it.

'Stay where you are—all of you! The game is up! Hand over the map and the millions!'

'I've never heard such cheek in all my days as a criminal,' exploded Herr Gustaffson. 'Who are you, anyway?'

'Your conqueror, Herr Gustaffson!' the woman answered. 'And yours, Agaton Sax!'

Herr Gustaffson threw down the map he was holding in his hand.

'Oh no, Herr Gustaffson,' said the woman scornfully, 'don't play games with me. You know as well as I do that that map is a forgery. You, Mr Sax, have the original. Give it to me, then I can give Herr Gustaffson my full attention while he counts up the fourteen million pounds he stole from me

'Stole from you!' Herr Gustaffson shouted angrily. 'I never stole anything from you—you are a liar as well as a thief!'

Agaton Sax calmly put his hand in his inside pocket, and produced the original map. He held it in front of the P.C.M.'s ever-open mouth, and delivered himself of the following momentous words:

'You are quite right, madam. The game is up. You are

the sister of the so-called Colossus of Rhodes, or so you wish us to believe. But I, Agaton Sax, know that you are none other than the Colossus himself. Exceptional intelligence, a cool head and a complete contempt for the feelings of other people have made it possible to steal the fourteen million pounds Herr Gustaffson has just helped himself to. I regret that I am unable to give you the map you would so dearly love to possess. The fact is that in a few moments it will no longer exist.'

So saying he held the map up once more, dangled it for a moment and then flicked it delicately into the mouth of the P.C.M., which, after a moment's vigorous mastication, transformed it into a greyish porridge.

The Colossus of Rhodes—for Agaton Sax was quite right, she really was the mysterious Colossus—bellowed with rage, and pointed her revolver at him threateningly.

'Be careful, she might shoot!' warned Lispington.

'Oh, no she won't,' Agaton Sax whispered back.

He had seen the door open again—swiftly and silently. The Colossus spun round—but was too late to defend herself against the onslaught of a flying yellow object. As it streaked through the air it seemed like some doom-laden thunderbolt but, in fact it was nothing more remarkable than a yellow plastic pail, thrust over her head with considerable speed and accuracy by whoever it was who had opened the door.

'It's your Aunt, Agaton!' gasped Lispington, shocked by the sudden appearance of Aunt Matilda, who had once upturned just such a pail on his own unsuspecting head, a disagreeable incident in his career which he preferred not to think about. For a few moments the room was in chaos. Agaton Sax seized the Colossus by the arms, Tickie barked furiously, and, small though she was, drove Herr Gustaffson's assistants back against the wall, where they were joined by Herr Gustaffson himself, now so scared that his teeth, too, were chattering. The whole gang raised their arms above their heads in a gesture of total surrender.

'Well done, Aunt!' exclaimed Agaton Sax. 'You got here in the nick of time!'

Suddenly the whole room was full of people—castle guards and policemen—all panting and shouting, and trying to arrest anybody and everybody, until Agaton Sax was able to explain patiently to them whom they should arrest and whom they shouldn't, who had committed the crimes and who had not, and so on.

'And keep a particularly sharp eye on Herr Gustaffson,' he added. 'Remember, he still has the fourteen million pounds he stole from the Colossus.'

He mopped his forehead, and turned to Aunt Matilda, who was sitting on the cannon ball and eyeing her nephew critically.

'Now, Agaton, please explain to me what you were doing when I arrived on the scene. Was it really necessary for you to hang on a rope like that? Especially as you are wearing your new travelling suit.'

'Perhaps you would like to tell me what you were doing down in the garden?' replied Agaton Sax with dignity. 'Why did you come to Rhodes and how did you get here?'

'Well, everything was so dull at home after you'd gone, so I bought myself a ticket for a packet tour, or whatever they call them. When I left my hotel an hour ago to look round this funny little town—whom should I meet but Tickie. As soon as I saw her I knew that you were up to your neck in trouble again, so I thought the best thing I could do was to go and buy a yellow plastic pail, in case any crooks decided to threaten me. You know I believe in self-defence. I picked up Tickie's lead and she dragged me along until we got to a large park. There was a crowd gathered there, and it occurred to me that they might all be villains because all the lights, all over the park, had been switched off and it was pitch dark. But I told myself I had nothing to worry about, because I had my pail if anyone tried to attack me. Suddenly, searchlights flooded the area with light, and I saw a high wall towering above me, with somebody clinging on to a long rope. Everybody began to shout, and point at the wall; I, of course, knew that the man on the rope was you, Agaton. I called your name and Tickie began to bark. She picked up a scent and dragged me towards the castle wall, up the stairs and on to the roof. We left the roof through a doorway and Tickie led me from one passage to another, all the time pulling and pulling. I told myself "Matilda you had better keep your eyes open. Agaton must have been kidnapped by a really big crook this time". At this point I found myself standing outside a closed door. I pushed it open, and saw that dreadful woman pointing her revolver at you. I said to myself, "Oh no you don't, you wicked creature; we've had enough of your dirty tricks, so I'll just adorn your fair head with this beautiful hat". And there she was, with a yellow pail stuck fast on her shoulders. The rest you know.'

'Fantastic!' murmured Lispington, who hadn't understood a word.

Almost moved to tears, Agaton Sax pressed his Aunt's hands warmly

The Commissioner of Police, Scotland Yard Division, arrived in Rhodes by air from London early the next morning, especially to arrange a banquet in honour of Agaton Sax, Lispington, and Aunt Matilda. Also invited to the banquet was the President of the *International Association for the Mutual Support and Assistance of Millionaires*

(IAMSAM), an immensely rich elderly gentleman who arrived in his private DC8-Super-Jet.

As the ice-cream was being served, Lispington leant over to his friend and whispered in his ear, 'Tell me, Agaton, was she really a *fhuinum*?'

'Oh, no,' said Agaton Sax. 'But she had followed Herr Gustaffson to Scotland Yard and seen where he kept you prisoner. She disguised herself as a cleaner, and set you free.'

'But why?'

'Because she wanted you to arrest Herr Gustaffson!'

'And the dentist?'

'The dentist. Well, he was the man we thought was the Colossus.'

'And what about *tlu nemxu*—the nurse, that is?'

'*Tlu nemxu* was the same person as *tlu fhuinum*—in other words, the nurse and the cleaner were one and the same person—the sister of the man we called The Colossus.

'Yes,' mused Lispington, 'she must have been The Colossus's assistant. I see it all now.'

'But you're wrong. She *was* The Colossus. He was simply her assistant.'

'How on earth did you work that out, Agaton?'

'Very easily! As soon as I saw the man, first in conference with Herr Gustaffson, then playing cards with him, I realized that he could not possibly have carried out the many masterly crimes which bore the name and signature, *Colossus of Rhodes*. Neither his intelligence nor his knowledge would have been up to it. So, he must have been acting as a tool for somebody else—somebody really brilliant, a genius in the world of crime. It came to me in a flash that the brains behind this big fellow belonged to his own sister.'

'But the game of cards!' exclaimed Lispington. 'Don't

forget that he won against a skilled cheat like Herr Gustaffson! It takes brains to do that, doesn't it?'

'But *he* didn't win the game! *She* did!'

'What!'

'Of course. It was a simple trick. You remember I had my walkie-talkie with me. I listened in on the whole game.'

'What!'

'His sister was hidden in a small room at the back of the hall. Just behind Herr Gustaffson. She could see his cards through a hole in the wall. She and her brother were in radio communication with each other throughout the game. She had a microphone, he had a tiny receiver in his ear. She told him exactly what cards Herr Gustaffson had in his hand, so it wasn't difficult for him to ask for the right one. It's an old trick. I've seen it done in films.'

'I never go to the cinema,' grunted Lispington. 'Just imagine how cunning and ruthless some people must be. Then what happened?'

'Then, you remember, you shadowed the gang in a taxi. I sneaked into the house where Herr Gustaffson and his gang had taken the Colossus after they had drugged him. At that point we were still calling him The Colossus.'

'What did you hope to find in there?'

'I was sure that his sister would follow Herr Gustaffson after he and his gang had drugged her brother and taken him to this other house. I saw her go in. It only took her a moment to find the room where they had dumped her brother. She managed to open the door, roused him by throwing a pail of cold water over him, and asked him where he kept his revolver? He murmured something about a bottom drawer, adding that it wasn't loaded, and that he had no cartridges. Then he dropped off to sleep again. I saw and heard everything, and watched her run off: doubtless going home to collect the unloaded revolver before rush-

ing to the castle, where it didn't take her long to track down Herr Gustaffson and his gang. She arrived at the precise moment when they had not only you, but also me in their power. Only they didn't really have me trapped, because I knew two things they didn't. I knew the revolver wasn't loaded and I knew Aunt Matilda and Tickie were coming to the rescue. You see when I was hanging from that rope I heard her call my name. Agaton is a Greek word meaning *happy*, which is why everyone thought she was talking Greek. I, my dear friend, I, Agaton Sax, am so happy we have been able to solve this case together.'

The banquet ended with a solemn ceremony, when the President of IAMSAM conferred the Grand Order of his Association (First Class) upon Agaton Sax and Lispington. Aunt Matilda, who had done as much as anyone to put the villains under lock and key, had to be content with a medal. Red tape prevented her from getting the honours she deserved—they could not be bestowed on a woman.